Taste of Home

FARMHOUSE FAMILY DINNERS

FARMHOUSE FAMILY DINNERS

TASTE OF HOME BOOKS • RDA ENTHUSIAST BRANDS, LLC • MILWAUKEE, WI

1610 N. 2nd St., Suite 102, Milwaukee, WI 53212-3906

Visit us at tasteofhome.com for other Taste of Home books and products.

ISBN: 978-1-62145-735-0
LOCC: 2021933638

Executive Editor: Mark Hagen
Senior Art Director: Raeann Thompson
Art Director: Maggie Conners
Deputy Editor, Copy Desk: Dulcie Shoener
Contributing Designer: Jennifer Ruetz
Contributing Copy Editor: Deb Warlaumont Mulvey

Cover
Photographer: Mark Derse
Set Stylist: Melissa Franco
Food Stylist: Shannon Norris

Pictured on title page: Balsamic Braised Pot Roast, p. 148

Pictured here: Franco family, p. 60; Italian Pinwheel Rolls, p. 103

Pictured on back cover: Mixed Fruit Shortcakes, p. 327; Girls walking, p. 266; Red, White & Blue Summer Salad, p. 244; Beth Howard, p. 151; Smoky Macaroni & Cheese, p. 272; Beef Tenderloin with Roasted Vegetables, p. 171; Stoney Acres Farm, p. 150

Printed in China
1 3 5 7 9 10 8 6 4 2

Cover Meal

- Citrus-Herb Roast Chicken, p. 196
- Chive Smashed Potatoes, p. 232
- Garden Salad with Chickpeas, p. 252
- Easy Batter Rolls, p. 228
- Strawberry Mascarpone Cake, p. 301

SERVE WITH:
Chicken Marsala Lasagna, Page 127

SETTLE IN FOR THE HEARTWARMING GOODNESS OF A FAMILY DINNER

Few things satisfy the soul like creating incredible kitchen-table memories with those you love most. From cozy weeknight suppers to unforgettable holiday celebrations, oven-fresh meals bring people together, filling homes with laughter, comfort and joy.

When it comes to the foods that are always sure to satisfy, farmhouse dishes rise to the top of everyone's list. Savory pot roasts, crispy fried chicken, buttery biscuits, finger-licking barbecue, garden-fresh sides and luscious berry pies...you'll find all of these down-home classics and so many others in the pages of *Farmhouse Family Dinners.*

Country cooks know that a homemade Sunday dinner simply can't be beat—no matter what day of the week it is. That's why they've shared their all-time best recipes in this must-have collection of 157 delicious dishes.

If you're looking to serve a farmhouse meal, you're in luck because these country cooks have done all the planning for you! Take a look inside and you'll see that this keepsake cookbook offers two ways to serve memory-making dinners.

The first half of this book features complete meals, such as a mouthwatering meat loaf super and a new take on taco Tuesday. You can also turn to page 332 for a menu planner that promises to address your dinnertime dilemmas. In fact, you'll find 46 complete menus in all.

You'll also enjoy chapters of country-kissed entrees, side dishes and desserts. See these sections to create your own supper, and watch for the "Serve With" callout for delicious pairings.

Gathering with family and friends has never been easier, tastier or more rewarding. Whether you are preparing a special weekend menu, setting the table after work or hosting a seasonal celebration, *Farmhouse Family Dinners* helps deliver the heartfelt memories that make your meals all the more special.

CONTENTS

CHAPTER 1

FARMHOUSE MENUS

The dinner table is a place to relax, regroup and reconnect. After all, few things bring families together like sharing a home-cooked meal at the end of the day. Here, you'll find 15 complete dinners ideal for weeknights, Sunday dinners and special occasions alike. Prepare one tonight, then settle in for the heartwarming comfort best found when surrounded by those you love most.

Hearty Ham Dinner
• Maple-Glazed Ham
• Citrus-Tarragon Asparagus Salad
• Overnight Yeast Rolls
• Refreshing Raspberry Iced Tea
• Chocolate & Coconut Cream Torte

MAPLE-GLAZED HAM

I cook this ham for Christmas and for Easter, but my husband thinks that twice a year is not enough. If it were up to him, we'd eat this every day! When I have larger hams, I double the glaze, which is also good on pancakes the next day.

—Jeanie Beasley, Tupelo, MS

PREP: 10 MIN. • **COOK:** 1¾ HOURS • **MAKES:** 15 SERVINGS

- **1 spiral-sliced fully cooked bone-in ham (7 to 9 lbs.)**

GLAZE

- **½ cup packed brown sugar**
- **½ cup maple syrup**
- **2 Tbsp. prepared mustard**
- **½ tsp. ground cinnamon**
- **¼ tsp. ground nutmeg**

1. Preheat oven to 300°. Place ham on a rack in a shallow roasting pan. Cover and bake until a thermometer reads 130°, 1½-2 hours.

2. Meanwhile, in a large saucepan, combine glaze ingredients. Bring to a boil; cook and stir until mixture is slightly thickened, 2-3 minutes.

3. Remove the ham from the oven. Pour glaze over the ham. Bake the ham, uncovered, until a thermometer reads 140°, 15-30 minutes longer.

4 OZ.: 234 cal., 6g fat (2g sat. fat), 93mg chol., 1137mg sod., 15g carb. (14g sugars, 0 fiber), 31g pro.

CITRUS-TARRAGON ASPARAGUS SALAD

I created this colorful salad when I was invited to a friend's picnic. The guests were begging to get my recipe. Letting the salad marinate in the fridge a few hours produces the best flavor.

—Cheryl Magnuson, Apple Valley, CA

PREP: 40 MIN. + CHILLING • **BROIL:** 15 MIN. • **MAKES:** 12 SERVINGS

3 medium sweet red peppers
3 lbs. fresh asparagus, trimmed
½ cup minced shallots

DRESSING
⅓ cup white balsamic vinegar
2 Tbsp. grated orange zest
2 Tbsp. minced fresh tarragon
1 Tbsp. honey
1 tsp. sea salt
¼ tsp. pepper
⅔ cup walnut or olive oil

1. Preheat broiler. Place peppers on a foil-lined baking sheet. Broil 4 in. from heat until skins blister, about 5 minutes. With tongs, rotate peppers a quarter turn. Broil and rotate until all sides are blistered and blackened. Immediately place peppers in a large bowl; let stand, covered, 20 minutes.

2. Meanwhile, in a 6-qt. stockpot, bring 8 cups water to a boil. Add asparagus in batches; cook, uncovered, just until crisp-tender, 1-2 minutes. Remove asparagus and immediately drop into ice water. Drain and pat dry; cut into halves.

3. Peel off and discard charred skin on peppers. Remove stems and seeds. Cut peppers into ¼-in.-wide strips. In a large bowl, combine asparagus, red peppers and shallots. For dressing, in a small bowl, whisk vinegar, orange zest, tarragon, honey, salt and pepper. Gradually whisk in oil until blended. Drizzle over asparagus mixture; toss to coat. Refrigerate up to 4 hours before serving, stirring occasionally.

¾ CUP: 148 cal., 12g fat (1g sat. fat), 0mg chol., 168mg sod., 9g carb. (6g sugars, 2 fiber), 2g pro.

DIABETIC EXCHANGES: 2½ fat, 1 vegetable.

OVERNIGHT YEAST ROLLS

It's easy to make light and flavorful rolls with this no-fuss recipe. The dough can also be used for cinnamon rolls, herb bread or coffee cake.

—Trisha Kruse, Eagle, ID

PREP: 20 MIN. + CHILLING • **BAKE:** 15 MIN. • **MAKES:** 2 DOZEN

- **1 Tbsp. sugar**
- **1 Tbsp. active dry yeast**
- **1½ tsp. salt**
- **5½ to 6 cups all-purpose flour**
- **1 cup buttermilk**
- **½ cup water**
- **½ cup butter, cubed**
- **3 large eggs, room temperature**
- **2 Tbsp. butter, melted**

1. In a large bowl, mix sugar, yeast, salt and 3 cups flour. In a small saucepan, heat buttermilk, water and ½ cup butter to 120°-130°. Add to dry ingredients; beat on medium speed 2 minutes. Add eggs; beat on high 2 minutes. Stir in enough remaining flour to form a soft dough (dough will be sticky).

2. Do not knead. Place dough in a large greased bowl. Cover; refrigerate overnight.

3. Punch down dough. Turn onto a lightly floured surface; divide and shape into 24 balls. Place 2 in. apart on greased baking sheets. Cover with kitchen towels; let rise in a warm place until almost doubled, about 1½ hours.

4. Preheat oven to 400°. Bake until rolls are golden brown, 15-20 minutes. Brush with melted butter. Remove from pans to wire racks; serve warm.

1 ROLL: 163 cal., 6g fat (3g sat. fat), 36mg chol., 215mg sod., 23g carb. (1g sugars, 1g fiber), 4g pro.

REFRESHING RASPBERRY ICED TEA

This recipe makes two gallons, so it's a sensible thirst-quenching choice for a springtime dinner when you have a medium-size crowd. It freezes well, too, making it a timesaver for party prep.

—Arlana Hendricks, Manchester, TN

PREP/TOTAL: 20 MIN. • **MAKES:** 16 SERVINGS

- **6 cups water**
- **1¾ cups sugar**
- **8 tea bags**
- **¾ cup frozen apple-raspberry juice concentrate**
- **8 cups cold water**
- **Ice cubes**
- **Fresh raspberries, optional**

In a large saucepan, bring 6 cups water and sugar to a boil; remove from heat. Add tea bags; steep, covered, 3-5 minutes according to taste. Discard tea bags. Add juice concentrate; stir in cold water. Serve over ice, with raspberries if desired.

1 CUP: 108 cal., 0 fat (0 sat. fat), 0 chol., 7mg sod., 28g carb. (27g sugars, 0 fiber), 0 pro.

CHOCOLATE & COCONUT CREAM TORTE

My grandmother passed this recipe down to me many years ago, and now I make it for my own grandchildren. When preparing this torte, make sure the chocolate layer is properly chilled before adding the next layer, or the coconut will sink into it.

—Jason Purkey, Ocean City, MD

PREP: 25 MIN. + CHILLING • **COOK:** 10 MIN. + STANDING • **MAKES:** 12 SERVINGS

- **1 pkg. (12 oz.) vanilla wafers, crushed**
- **½ cup butter, melted**
- **8 oz. dark baking chocolate, chopped**
- **1 cup heavy whipping cream**

FILLING

- **1 can (13½ oz.) coconut milk**
- **3 cups sweetened shredded coconut**
- **1 cup sugar**
- **2 Tbsp. cornstarch**
- **4 Tbsp. cold water, divided**
- **1 large egg**
- **1 large egg yolk**
- **2 tsp. unflavored gelatin**
- **1¼ cups heavy whipping cream**
- **½ cup sweetened shredded coconut, toasted**

1. In a large bowl, mix wafer crumbs and butter. Press onto bottom and 2 in. up sides of a greased 9-in. springform pan.

2. Place chocolate in a small bowl. In a small saucepan, bring 1 cup cream just to a boil. Pour cream over the chocolate; let stand 5 minutes. Stir with a whisk until smooth. Pour over prepared crust. Refrigerate 1 hour.

3. In a large saucepan, combine coconut milk, coconut and sugar; bring just to a boil. Strain through a fine-mesh strainer into a bowl, reserving strained coconut; return coconut milk mixture to saucepan. In a small bowl, mix cornstarch and 2 Tbsp. water until smooth; stir into coconut milk mixture. Return to a boil, stirring constantly; cook and stir until thickened, 1-2 minutes. Remove from heat.

4. In a small bowl, whisk egg and egg yolk. Whisk a small amount of hot mixture into egg mixture; return all to pan, whisking constantly. Bring to a gentle boil; cook and stir 2 minutes. Remove from heat.

5. In a microwave-safe bowl, sprinkle the gelatin over the remaining cold water; let stand 1 minute. Microwave on high for 30-40 seconds. Stir and let stand until gelatin is completely dissolved, about 1 minute. Whisk gelatin mixture into coconut milk mixture. Refrigerate, covered, 1 hour, whisking every 15 minutes.

6. In a large bowl, beat cream until stiff peaks form; fold into coconut milk mixture. Spoon reserved strained coconut into prepared crust. Spread filling over coconut. Refrigerate 6 hours or overnight before serving.

7. Remove rim from pan. Top with toasted coconut.

1 PIECE: 691 cal., 49g fat (32g sat. fat), 107mg chol., 265mg sod., 63g carb. (49g sugars, 3g fiber), 6g pro.

Fried-Chicken Sunday Dinner

- Best-Ever Fried Chicken
- Traditional Mashed Potatoes
- Kale Caesar Salad
- Southern Buttermilk Biscuits

BEST-EVER FRIED CHICKEN

Family reunions and neighborly gatherings will never be the same when you serve this crispy, juicy and perfectly seasoned fried chicken. I grew up on a farm and every year when it was time to bale hay, my dad would hire farm hands to help. The crew looked forward to coming because they knew they would be treated to my mom's delicious fried chicken.

—Lola Clifton, Vinton, VA

PREP: 15 MIN. • **COOK:** 20 MIN. • **MAKES:** 4 SERVINGS

- **1¾ cups all-purpose flour**
- **1 Tbsp. dried thyme**
- **1 Tbsp. paprika**
- **2 tsp. salt**
- **2 tsp. garlic powder**
- **1 tsp. pepper**
- **1 large egg**
- **⅓ cup 2% milk**
- **2 Tbsp. lemon juice**
- **1 broiler/fryer chicken (3 to 4 lbs.), cut up**
- **Oil for deep-fat frying**

1. In a shallow bowl, mix the first 6 ingredients. In a separate shallow bowl, whisk egg, milk and lemon juice until blended. Dip chicken in flour mixture to coat all sides; shake off excess. Dip in egg mixture, then again in flour mixture.

2. In an electric skillet or deep fryer, heat oil to 375°. Fry the chicken, a few pieces at a time, for 6-10 minutes on each side or until skin is golden brown and juices run clear. Drain on paper towels.

1 SERVING: 811 cal., 57g fat (9g sat. fat), 176mg chol., 725mg sod., 26g carb. (2g sugars, 2g fiber), 47g pro.

TRADITIONAL MASHED POTATOES

Mashed potatoes go with just about any meal, so you may want to keep this recipe handy. We like to use good ol' russets or Yukon Golds.

—Taste of Home *Test Kitchen*

TAKES: 30 MIN. • **MAKES:** 6 SERVINGS (ABOUT 4½ CUPS)

- **6 medium russet potatoes (about 2 lbs.), peeled and cubed**
- **½ cup warm whole milk or heavy whipping cream**
- **¼ cup butter, cubed**
- **¾ tsp. salt**
- **Dash pepper**

Place potatoes in a large saucepan; add water to cover. Bring to a boil. Reduce heat to medium; cook, uncovered, until easily pierced with a fork, 20-25 minutes. Drain. Add the remaining ingredients; mash until light and fluffy.

¾ CUP: 168 cal., 8g fat (5g sat. fat), 22mg chol., 367mg sod., 22g carb. (3g sugars, 1g fiber), 3g pro.

KALE CAESAR SALAD

I love Caesar salad recipes, so I created this version with kale. It's perfect paired with chicken or steak for a great family meal.

—Rashanda Cobbins, Milwaukee, Wisconsin

TAKES: 15 MIN. • **MAKES:** 8 SERVINGS

- **4 cups chopped fresh kale**
- **4 cups torn romaine**
- **1 cup Caesar salad croutons**
- **½ cup shredded Parmesan cheese**
- **½ cup mayonnaise**
- **2 Tbsp. lemon juice**
- **1 Tbsp. Worcestershire sauce**
- **2 tsp. Dijon mustard**
- **2 tsp. anchovy paste**
- **1 garlic clove, minced**
- **¼ tsp. salt**
- **¼ tsp. pepper**

In a large salad bowl, toss kale, romaine, croutons and cheese. For dressing, combine remaining ingredients in a small bowl; pour over the salad and toss to coat. Serve immediately.

1 CUP: 148 cal., 13g fat (3g sat. fat), 10mg chol., 417mg sod., 6g carb., (1g sugars, 1g fiber), 3g.

DIABETIC EXCHANGES: 2½ fat, 1 vegetable.

SOUTHERN BUTTERMILK BISCUITS

The recipe for these four-ingredient biscuits has been handed down for many generations.

—Fran Thompson, Tarboro, NC

CHAPTER 1

TAKES: 30 MIN. • **MAKES:** 8 BISCUITS

½ cup cold butter, cubed
2 cups self-rising flour
¾ cup buttermilk
Melted butter

1. In a large bowl, cut butter into flour until mixture resembles coarse crumbs. Stir in buttermilk just until moistened. Turn onto a lightly floured surface; knead 3-4 times. Pat or lightly roll to ¾-in. thickness. Cut with a floured 2½-in. biscuit cutter.

2. Place on a greased baking sheet. Bake at 425° until golden brown, 11-13 minutes. Brush tops with butter. Serve warm.

1 BISCUIT: 222 cal., 12g fat (7g sat. fat), 31mg chol., 508mg sod., 24g carb. (1g sugars, 1g fiber), 4g pro.

Farmhouse Turkey
• Juicy Roast Turkey
• Moist Turkey Sausage Stuffing
• Almond Broccoli Salad
• Southern Sweet Potato Tart

JUICY ROAST TURKEY

I can't wait to serve this juicy turkey at Thanksgiving—so I make it several times a year. The aroma that wafts through the house during baking is almost as mouthwatering as the turkey dinner itself.

—Terrie Herman, North Myrtle Beach, SC

PREP: 20 MIN. + CHILLING • **BAKE:** 3½ HOURS + STANDING • **MAKES:** 12 SERVINGS

- **¼ cup ground mustard**
- **2 Tbsp. Worcestershire sauce**
- **2 Tbsp. olive oil**
- **½ tsp. white vinegar**
- **1 tsp. salt**
- **⅛ tsp. pepper**
- **1 turkey (10 to 12 lbs.)**
- **1 medium onion, quartered**
- **2 celery ribs, quartered lengthwise**
- **Fresh parsley sprigs**
- **2 bacon strips**
- **¼ cup butter, softened**
- **2 cups chicken broth**
- **1 cup water**

1. In a small bowl, combine the first 6 ingredients. Brush over turkey. Place the turkey on a platter. Cover and refrigerate for 1-24 hours.

2. Preheat oven to 325°. Place turkey on a rack in a shallow roasting pan, breast side up. Add the onion, celery and parsley to turkey cavity. Tuck wings under turkey; tie drumsticks together. Arrange bacon over top of turkey breast. Spread butter over turkey. Pour broth and water into pan.

3. Bake, uncovered, until a thermometer inserted in the thickest part of thigh reads 170°-175°, 3½-4 hours, basting occasionally. Remove the turkey from oven. If desired, remove and discard bacon. Tent with foil; let stand 20 minutes before carving. If desired, skim fat and thicken pan drippings for gravy. Serve with turkey.

8 OZ. COOKED TURKEY: 535 cal., 29g fat (9g sat. fat), 219mg chol., 594mg sod., 2g carb. (1g sugars, 0 fiber), 62g pro.

MOIST TURKEY SAUSAGE STUFFING

With tangy apricots and turkey sausage, this stuffing is a terrific mix of sweet and savory.

—Priscilla Gilbert, Indian Harbour Beach, FL

PREP: 20 MIN. • **COOK:** 20 MIN. • **MAKES:** 16 SERVINGS

- **1 pkg. (19½ oz.) Italian turkey sausage links, casings removed**
- **4 celery ribs, chopped**
- **1 large onion, chopped**
- **1½ cups chopped dried apricots**
- **¼ cup minced fresh parsley**
- **1 Tbsp. minced fresh sage or 1 tsp. dried sage**
- **1 tsp. poultry seasoning**
- **¼ tsp. pepper**
- **3¼ cups chicken stock**
- **1 pkg. (12 oz.) crushed cornbread stuffing**
- **1 cup fresh or frozen cranberries, chopped**

1. In a Dutch oven, cook the turkey sausage, celery and onion over medium heat until meat is no longer pink and vegetables are tender, breaking sausage into crumbles; drain. Stir in the apricots, parsley, sage, poultry seasoning and pepper; cook 3 minutes longer.

2. Add stock; bring to a boil. Stir in the cornbread stuffing; cook and stir until liquid is absorbed. Gently stir in the cranberries; heat through.

⅔ CUP: 176 cal., 3g fat (1g sat. fat), 13mg chol., 540mg sod., 30g carb. (8g sugars, 3g fiber), 7g pro.

DIABETIC EXCHANGES: 2 starch, 1 lean meat.

ALMOND BROCCOLI SALAD

This colorful salad is easy to make, and I like that it can be prepared ahead. Add the almonds and bacon just before serving so they stay nice and crunchy.

—Margaret Garbade, Tulsa, OK

TAKES: 25 MIN. • **MAKES:** 12 SERVINGS

- **1 bunch broccoli (about 1½ lbs.)**
- **1 cup mayonnaise**
- **¼ cup red wine vinegar**
- **2 Tbsp. sugar**
- **¼ tsp. salt**
- **½ tsp. freshly ground pepper**
- **1 pkg. (7 oz.) mixed dried fruit**
- **¼ cup finely chopped red onion**
- **1 pkg. (2¼ oz.) slivered almonds, toasted**
- **4 bacon strips, cooked and crumbled**

1. Cut florets from broccoli, reserving stalks; cut florets into 1-in. pieces. Using a paring knife, remove peel from thick stalks; cut stalks into ½-in. pieces.

2. In a small bowl, mix mayonnaise, vinegar, sugar, salt and pepper. In a large bowl, combine broccoli, dried fruit and onion. Add mayonnaise mixture; toss to coat. Refrigerate until serving.

3. Just before serving, sprinkle with almonds and bacon.

¾ CUP: 236 cal., 17g fat (3g sat. fat), 1mg chol., 180mg sod., 21g carb. (15g sugars, 3g fiber), 3g pro.

SOUTHERN SWEET POTATO TART

We love sweet potatoes, so I try to incorporate them in as many dishes as I can. My secret ingredient is the bourbon—it's what makes it so delicious.

—Marie Bruno, Watkinsville, GA

PREP: 1 HOUR • **BAKE:** 25 MIN. + COOLING • **MAKES:** 8 SERVINGS

1 lb. sweet potatoes (about 2 small)
Pastry for single-crust pie
¼ cup butter, softened
½ cup packed dark brown sugar
2 Tbsp. all-purpose flour
1 tsp. pumpkin pie spice
¼ tsp. salt
1 large egg, room temperature
¼ cup heavy whipping cream
1 Tbsp. bourbon or 1 Tbsp. whipping cream plus ½ tsp. vanilla extract

TOPPING

2 Tbsp. butter, softened
2 Tbsp. dark brown sugar
2 Tbsp. dark corn syrup
½ cup chopped pecans

1. Preheat oven to 400°. Place potatoes on a foil-lined baking sheet. Bake until tender, 40-50 minutes.

2. On a lightly floured surface, roll dough to a ⅛-in.-thick circle; transfer to a 9-in. tart pan with removable bottom. Press onto bottom and sides of pan; trim edges to edge of pan. Refrigerate while preparing filling.

3. Remove potatoes from oven; increase oven setting to 425°. When potatoes are cool enough to handle, remove peel and place pulp in a large bowl; beat until smooth (you will need 1 cup mashed). Add butter, brown sugar, flour, pie spice and salt; beat until blended. Beat in egg, cream and bourbon. Pour into crust. Bake on a lower oven rack 15 minutes.

4. Meanwhile, for topping, mix butter, brown sugar and corn syrup until blended. Stir in pecans.

5. Remove pie; reduce oven setting to 350°. Spoon topping evenly over pie. Bake until a knife inserted in the center comes out clean, 8-10 minutes.

6. Cool on a wire rack. Serve within 2 hours or refrigerate, covered, and serve cold.

1 PIECE: 477 cal., 29g fat (15g sat. fat), 85mg chol., 326mg sod., 52g carb. (27g sugars, 3g fiber), 5g pro.

PASTRY FOR SINGLE-CRUST PIE: Combine 1¼ cups all-purpose flour and ¼ tsp. salt; cut in ½ cup cold butter until crumbly. Gradually add 3-5 Tbsp. ice water, tossing with a fork until the dough holds together when pressed. Wrap and refrigerate 1 hour.

Casual Comforts
• Chicken Cordon Bleu Pasta
• Spinach Salad with Poppy Seed Dressing
• Whole Wheat French Bread
• Sparkling Cider Pound Cake

CHICKEN CORDON BLEU PASTA

Fans of my blog, *Chef in Training*, inspired me to create this creamy pasta casserole out of ingredients I had on hand. Success! I took the dish for another flavorful spin and added a bit of smoky bacon and toasted bread crumbs.

—Nikki Barton, Providence, UT

PREP: 25 MIN. • **BAKE:** 20 MIN. • **MAKES:** 6 SERVINGS

- **3 cups uncooked penne pasta**
- **2 cups heavy whipping cream**
- **1 pkg. (8 oz.) cream cheese, softened and cubed**
- **1½ cups shredded Swiss cheese, divided**
- **½ tsp. onion powder**
- **½ tsp. garlic salt**
- **¼ tsp. pepper**
- **3 cups sliced cooked chicken breasts**
- **¾ cup crumbled cooked bacon**
- **¾ cup cubed fully cooked ham**
- **3 Tbsp. dry bread crumbs**

1. Preheat oven to 350°. Cook pasta according to package directions for al dente.

2. Meanwhile, in a large saucepan, heat cream and cream cheese over medium heat until smooth, stirring occasionally. Stir in 1 cup Swiss cheese, onion powder, garlic salt and pepper until blended.

3. Drain pasta; stir in chicken, bacon and ham. Add sauce; toss to coat. Transfer to a greased 13x9-in. baking dish. Sprinkle with remaining cheese and the bread crumbs. Bake, uncovered, 18-22 minutes or until heated through.

1½ CUPS: 826 cal., 56g fat (33g sat. fat), 249mg chol., 1093mg sod., 33g carb. (3g sugars, 1g fiber), 47g pro.

SPINACH SALAD WITH POPPY SEED DRESSING

I love to bring this salad to parties or serve it as a healthy lunch. It's been a family favorite for a while. The easy homemade dressing is the best part.
—Nikki Barton, Providence, UT

TAKES: 25 MIN. • **MAKES:** 6 SERVINGS (1 CUP DRESSING)

- **4 cups fresh baby spinach**
- **4 cups torn iceberg lettuce**
- **1½ cups sliced fresh mushrooms**
- **½ lb. bacon strips, cooked and crumbled**

DRESSING

- **¼ cup red wine vinegar**
- **¼ cup chopped red onion**
- **3 Tbsp. sugar**
- **¾ tsp. salt**
- **¼ tsp. ground mustard**
- **½ cup canola oil**
- **1½ tsp. poppy seeds**

1. In a large bowl, combine spinach, lettuce, mushrooms and bacon. Place vinegar, onion, sugar, salt and mustard in blender. While processing, gradually add oil in a steady stream. Transfer to a bowl; stir in poppy seeds.

2. Divide salad among 6 plates; drizzle with dressing.

1½ CUPS SALAD WITH ABOUT 2 TBSP. DRESSING: 280 cal., 24g fat (3g sat. fat), 14mg chol., 557mg sod., 10g carb. (8g sugars, 1g fiber), 6g pro.

WHOLE WHEAT FRENCH BREAD

The first time I made this recipe my husband asked if it was homemade or store-bought. When he reached for a second piece, I knew I had a winning recipe.

—Roseann Loker, Colon, MI

PREP: 25 MIN. + RISING • **BAKE:** 35 MIN. • **MAKES:** 2 LOAVES

5 to 5¼ cups all-purpose flour
2 cups stone-ground whole wheat flour
2 pkg. (¼ oz. each) active dry yeast
2½ cups water
1 Tbsp. sugar
1 Tbsp. salt
1 Tbsp. butter
Yellow cornmeal
1 large egg white
1 Tbsp. water

1. Combine the flours. In a large bowl, combine 3 cups flour mixture and the yeast. Set aside. Heat water, sugar, salt and butter to 115°-120°. Add to flour and yeast. Beat on low speed for 30 seconds; increase speed to medium and beat 3 minutes longer. Stir in enough remaining flour to make a soft dough.

2. Turn onto a lightly floured surface; knead until smooth and elastic, 6-8 minutes. Place dough in a greased bowl, turning once to grease the top. Cover and allow to rise in a warm place until doubled, about 1 hour.

3. Punch dough down; divide in half and let rest 10 minutes. Roll each half into a 15x12-in. rectangle. Roll up jelly-roll style, starting with the long side. Pinch seal and turn ends under to form a smooth loaf. Sprinkle 2 baking sheets with cornmeal and place each loaf, seam side down, on a greased baking sheet. Make slashes every 2½ in. in the top of each loaf. Cover and let rise until doubled, about 1 hour.

4. Beat the egg white and water; brush some over the loaves. Refrigerate remaining mixture. Bake at 375° for 20 minutes. Brush the loaves again with egg white mixture and bake 15-20 minutes longer or until golden brown. Remove pans to wire racks to cool.

1 SLICE: 102 cal., 1g fat (0 sat. fat), 1mg chol., 227mg sod., 21g carb. (1g sugars, 1g fiber), 3g pro.

SPARKLING CIDER POUND CAKE

This pound cake is incredible and completely reminds me of fall with every bite. Using sparkling apple cider in the batter and the glaze gives it a delicious and unique flavor. I love everything about it!

—Nikki Barton, Providence, UT

PREP: 20 MIN. • **BAKE:** 40 MIN. + COOLING • **MAKES:** 12 SERVINGS

- **¾ cup butter, softened**
- **1½ cups sugar**
- **3 large eggs, room temperature**
- **1½ cups all-purpose flour**
- **¼ tsp. baking powder**
- **¼ tsp. salt**
- **½ cup sparkling apple cider**

GLAZE

- **¾ cup confectioners' sugar**
- **3 to 4 tsp. sparkling apple cider**

1. Preheat oven to 350°. Line bottom of a greased 9x5-in. loaf pan with parchment; grease parchment.

2. In a large bowl, cream butter and sugar until light and fluffy, 5-7 minutes. Add eggs, 1 at a time, beating well after each addition. In another bowl, whisk flour, baking powder and salt; add to creamed mixture alternately with cider, beating well after each addition.

3. Transfer to prepared pan. Bake 40-50 minutes or until a toothpick inserted in center comes out clean. Cool in pan 10 minutes before removing to a wire rack to cool completely.

4. In a small bowl, mix glaze ingredients until smooth; spoon over top of cake, allowing it to flow over sides.

1 SLICE: 308 cal., 13g fat (8g sat. fat), 77mg chol., 169mg sod., 46g carb. (34g sugars, 0 fiber), 3g pro.

BRINGING THE FAMILY TOGETHER

For food blogger Nikki Barton, sharing a family meal is a top priority. "We try to sit down to home-cooked meals often," she says. "It's a great time to share our day. Best of all, the kids really open up when we are all together, and a lot of my fondest conversations actually occurred at our dinner table."

Family meals were key in Nikki's childhood home, too. "I remember watching Mom cook and thinking, *Cooking is not only fun, but it brings people together*."

After Nikki married her husband, Derek, she realized she needed to amp up her cooking skills. "I was overwhelmed with how I was going to cook for him," she explains.

"My grandma gave me collections of family recipes. When I put my own spins on them, they became popular at my home and with friends and extended family. That's when I began my own food blog, *www.chef-in-training.com*.

"It's a spot for anyone who wants to learn how to serve family meals," she adds. "I want people to learn to cook and develop a true passion for the kitchen."

Nikki instilled an interest for cooking in her little ones, too. "My kids love helping," she says. "They like eating what they've prepared, making it easier to get them to eat veggies. They also help plan our weekly dinner calendar. This gets them excited about dinner."

The Bartons don't plan on skipping family meals any time soon, Nikki says: "Home-cooked dinners bring us a measure of warmth, not only to our tummies, but to our hearts as well."

BARTON FAMILY PHOTO: SANDY DEGASSER

Nikki Barton serves up food and fun for her husband, Derek, and children (from left) Avrie, Grant and Jace.

Soup & Salad Supper
• Broccoli Beer Cheese Soup
• Roasted Apple Salad with Spicy Maple-Cider Vinaigrette
• Caraway Cheese Bread
• Autumn Apple Torte

BROCCOLI BEER CHEESE SOUP

Whether you include the beer or not, this soup tastes wonderful. I always make extra and pop individual servings into the freezer.

—Lori Lee, Brooksville, FL

PREP: 20 MIN. • **COOK:** 30 MIN. • **MAKES:** 10 SERVINGS (2½ QT.)

- **3 Tbsp. butter**
- **5 celery ribs, finely chopped**
- **3 medium carrots, finely chopped**
- **1 small onion, finely chopped**
- **4 cups fresh broccoli florets, chopped**
- **¼ cup chopped sweet red pepper**
- **4 cans (14½ oz. each) chicken broth**
- **½ tsp. pepper**
- **½ cup all-purpose flour**
- **½ cup water**
- **3 cups shredded cheddar cheese**
- **1 pkg. (8 oz.) cream cheese, cubed**
- **1 bottle (12 oz.) beer or nonalcoholic beer**
- **Optional toppings: Additional shredded cheddar cheese, cooked and crumbled bacon strips, chopped green onions, sour cream and salad croutons**

1. In a Dutch oven, melt butter over medium-high heat. Add celery, carrots and onion; saute until crisp-tender. Add broccoli and red pepper; stir in broth and pepper. Combine flour and water until smooth; gradually stir into pan. Bring to a boil. Reduce heat; simmer, uncovered, until soup is thickened and vegetables are tender, 25-30 minutes.

2. Stir in cheeses and beer until cheeses are melted (do not boil). Top with additional shredded cheese, bacon, green onions, sour cream and croutons as desired.

FREEZE OPTION: Before adding toppings, cool soup; transfer to freezer containers. Freeze up to 3 months. To use, partially thaw in refrigerator overnight; heat through in a large saucepan over medium-low heat, stirring occasionally (do not boil). Add toppings as desired.

1 CUP: 316 cal., 23g fat (13g sat. fat), 69mg chol., 1068mg sod., 13g carb. (5g sugars, 2g fiber), 12g pro.

ROASTED APPLE SALAD WITH SPICY MAPLE-CIDER VINAIGRETTE

We bought loads of apples and needed to use them. To help the flavors come alive, I roasted the apples and tossed them with a sweet dressing.

—Janice Elder, Charlotte, NC

PREP: 15 MIN. • **BAKE:** 20 MIN. + COOLING • **MAKES:** 8 SERVINGS

- **4 medium Fuji, Gala or other firm apples, quartered**
- **2 Tbsp. olive oil**

DRESSING

- **2 Tbsp. cider vinegar**
- **2 Tbsp. olive oil**
- **1 Tbsp. maple syrup**
- **1 tsp. Sriracha chili sauce**
- **½ tsp. salt**
- **¼ tsp. pepper**

SALAD

- **1 pkg. (5 oz.) spring mix salad greens**
- **4 pitted dates, quartered**
- **1 log (4 oz.) fresh goat cheese, crumbled**
- **½ cup chopped pecans, toasted**

1. Preheat oven to 375°. Place apples in a foil-lined 15x10x1-in. baking pan; drizzle with oil and toss to coat. Roast apples 20-30 minutes or until tender, stirring occasionally. Cool the apples completely.

2. In a small bowl, whisk dressing ingredients until blended. In a large bowl, combine salad greens and dates. Drizzle dressing over salad and toss to coat.

3. Divide mixture among 8 plates. Top with goat cheese and roasted apples; sprinkle with pecans. Serve immediately.

1 CUP: 191 cal., 13g fat (3g sat. fat), 9mg chol., 240mg sod., 17g carb. (12g sugars, 3g fiber), 3g pro.

DIABETIC EXCHANGES: 2 fat, 1 vegetable, ½ fruit.

CARAWAY CHEESE BREAD

We enjoy cheese in a variety of ways. In this savory bread, cheddar cheese blends beautifully with just the right amount of caraway.

—Homer Wooten, Ridgetown, ON

PREP: 10 MIN. • **BAKE:** 30 MIN. + COOLING • **MAKES:** 1 LOAF (16 SLICES)

2½ cups all-purpose flour
2 cups shredded cheddar cheese
1½ to 2 tsp. caraway seeds
¾ tsp. salt
½ tsp. baking powder
½ tsp. baking soda
2 large eggs, room temperature
1 cup plain yogurt
½ cup butter, melted
1 Tbsp. Dijon mustard

1. Preheat oven to 375°. In a large bowl, combine the first 6 ingredients. In another bowl, combine the remaining ingredients. Stir into dry ingredients just until moistened.

2. Pour into a greased 9x5-in. loaf pan. Bake until a toothpick comes out clean, 30-35 minutes. Cool 10 minutes before removing from pan to a wire rack. Serve bread warm. Refrigerate leftovers.

1 SLICE: 199 cal., 12g fat (7g sat. fat), 55mg chol., 338mg sod., 16g carb. (1g sugars, 1g fiber), 7g pro.

AUTUMN APPLE TORTE

When it's apple season, I always look forward to making this yummy torte with a cream cheese layer and apples galore.

—Margaret Wilson, San Bernardino, CA

PREP: 40 MIN. • **BAKE:** 35 MIN. + COOLING • **MAKES:** 12 SERVINGS

- **½ cup butter, softened**
- **½ cup sugar, divided**
- **½ tsp. vanilla extract**
- **1 cup all-purpose flour**
- **1 pkg. (8 oz.) cream cheese, softened**
- **1 large egg, room temperature, lightly beaten**
- **½ tsp. almond extract**
- **2 cups thinly sliced, peeled Granny Smith apples (about 2 medium)**
- **2 cups thinly sliced, peeled Cortland apples (about 2 medium)**
- **¼ cup cinnamon sugar**
- **¼ tsp. ground nutmeg**
- **½ cup confectioners' sugar**
- **2 Tbsp. 2% milk**
- **2 Tbsp. sliced almonds, toasted**

1. Preheat oven to 450°. In a small bowl, cream butter and ¼ cup sugar until light and fluffy, 5-7 minutes. Beat in vanilla. Gradually beat in flour. Press onto bottom and 1 in. up sides of a greased 9-in. springform pan.

2. In a small bowl, beat cream cheese and remaining sugar until smooth. Add egg and almond extract; beat on low speed just until blended. Pour into crust.

3. Place apples in a large bowl. Mix cinnamon sugar and nutmeg; add to apples and toss to coat. Arrange over cream cheese mixture. Bake 5 minutes.

4. Reduce oven setting to 400°. Bake until apples are tender, 30-35 minutes longer. Cool on a wire rack.

5. Remove rim from pan. In a small bowl, mix confectioners' sugar and milk until smooth. Drizzle over torte; sprinkle with almonds. Refrigerate leftovers.

1 SLICE: 270 cal., 15g fat (9g sat. fat), 57mg chol., 136mg sod., 31g carb. (22g sugars, 1g fiber), 3g pro.

Low Country Boil
• Frogmore Stew
• Oven-Fried Cornbread
• Sweet Tea Boysenberry Shandy
• Favorite Chocolate-Bourbon Pecan Tart

FROGMORE STEW

This picnic-style medley of shrimp, smoked kielbasa, corn and spuds is a specialty of South Carolina cuisine. It's commonly dubbed Frogmore stew or Beaufort stew in recognition of both of the low country communities that lay claim to its origin. No matter what you call it, this one-pot wonder won't disappoint!

—Taste of Home *Test Kitchen*

PREP: 10 MIN. • **COOK:** 35 MIN. • **MAKES:** 8 SERVINGS

16 cups water
1 large sweet onion, quartered
3 Tbsp. seafood seasoning
2 medium lemons, halved, optional
1 lb. small red potatoes
1 lb. smoked kielbasa or fully cooked hot links, cut into 1-in. pieces
4 medium ears sweet corn, cut into thirds
2 lbs. uncooked medium shrimp, peeled and deveined
Seafood cocktail sauce
Melted butter
Additional seafood seasoning

1. In a stockpot, combine water, onion, seafood seasoning and, if desired, lemons; bring to a boil. Add potatoes; cook, uncovered, 10 minutes. Add kielbasa and corn; return to a boil. Reduce heat; simmer, uncovered, 10-12 minutes or until potatoes are tender. Add shrimp; cook 2-3 minutes longer or until shrimp turn pink.

2. Drain; transfer to a bowl. Serve with cocktail sauce, butter and additional seasoning.

1 SERVING: 369 cal., 18g fat (6g sat. fat), 175mg chol., 751mg sod., 24g carb. (7g sugars, 2g fiber), 28g pro.

OVEN-FRIED CORNBREAD

Nothing says good southern cooking like a crisp cornbread baked in a cast-iron skillet. This is an old family recipe that has been passed down to each generation.

—Emory Doty, Jasper, GA

PREP: 20 MIN. • **BAKE:** 15 MIN. • **MAKES:** 8 SERVINGS

- **4 Tbsp. canola oil, divided**
- **1½ cups finely ground white cornmeal**
- **¼ cup sugar**
- **2 tsp. baking powder**
- **1 tsp. baking soda**
- **1 tsp. salt**
- **2 large eggs, room temperature**
- **2 cups buttermilk**

1. Place 2 Tbsp. oil in a 10-in. cast-iron skillet; place in oven. Preheat oven to 450°. Whisk together cornmeal, sugar, baking powder, baking soda and salt. In another bowl, whisk together eggs, buttermilk and remaining oil. Add to cornmeal mixture; stir just until moistened.

2. Carefully remove hot skillet from oven. Add batter; bake until golden brown and a toothpick inserted in center comes out clean, 15-20 minutes. Cut into wedges; serve warm.

1 PIECE: 238 cal., 9g fat (1g sat. fat), 49mg chol., 709mg sod., 33g carb. (10g sugars, 1g fiber), 6g pro.

SWEET TEA BOYSENBERRY SHANDY

I love an ice-cold beer on a hot summer day. I also love sweet tea, so one day I got the great idea to mix the two. Wow! It was absolutely delish. I experimented with different flavorings, and this combination was my favorite. Set aside some tea for the kids before stirring in the beer.

—Kelly Williams, Forked River, NJ

PREP: 10 MIN. • **COOK:** 5 MIN. + CHILLING • **MAKES:** 12 SERVINGS (2¼ QT.)

- **1½ cups water**
- **4 tea bags**
- **¾ cup sugar**
- **¾ cup boysenberry syrup**
- **4 cups cold water**
- **3 bottles (12 oz. each) beer or white ale, chilled**
- **1 medium orange, sliced, optional**

1. In a large saucepan, bring water to a boil; remove from heat. Add tea bags; steep, covered, 3-5 minutes, according to taste. Discard tea bags. Stir in sugar and syrup until dissolved. Stir in cold water. Transfer to a 3-qt. pitcher; refrigerate until cold.

2. Stir beer into tea mixture; serve immediately. If desired, top with orange slices.

¾ CUP: 137 cal., 0 fat (0 sat. fat), 0 chol., 5mg sod., 29g carb. (26g sugars, 0 fiber), 0 pro.

FAVORITE CHOCOLATE-BOURBON PECAN TART

I grew up in Louisiana, where, as in most of the South, pecan pie is a staple. When I tasted my first chocolate pecan pie, it blew my mind! I decided to boost the decadence of this dessert by adding bourbon, a great complement for the chocolate, and drizzling caramel on top.

—Amber Needham, San Antonio, TX

PREP: 15 MIN. • **BAKE:** 30 MIN. + COOLING • **MAKES:** 12 SERVINGS

- **Pastry for single-crust pie (9 in.)**
- **½ cup semisweet chocolate chips**
- **2 large eggs, room temperature**
- **¾ cup dark corn syrup**
- **½ cup sugar**
- **¼ cup butter, melted**
- **2 Tbsp. bourbon**
- **¼ tsp. salt**
- **1 cup pecan halves, toasted**
- **¼ cup hot caramel ice cream topping**

1. Preheat oven to 375°. On a lightly floured surface, roll dough to a 12-in. circle. Press onto the bottom and up sides of an ungreased 11-in. tart pan with removable bottom. Sprinkle with chocolate chips.

2. Beat eggs, corn syrup, sugar, butter, bourbon and salt. Stir in pecans. Pour over chocolate chips. Bake until center is just set and crust is golden brown, 30-35 minutes.

3. Cool on a wire rack. Cut into slices. Serve with hot caramel ice cream topping.

1 PIECE: 357 cal., 20g fat (9g sat. fat), 61mg chol., 250mg sod., 43g carb. (32g sugars, 2g fiber), 4g pro.

PASTRY FOR SINGLE-CRUST PIE: Combine 1¼ cups all-purpose flour and ¼ tsp. salt; cut in ½ cup cold butter until crumbly. Gradually add 3-5 Tbsp. ice water, tossing with a fork until the dough holds together when pressed. Cover and refrigerate 1 hour.

KITCHEN TIP: To toast nuts, bake in a shallow pan in a 350° oven for 5-10 minutes or cook in a skillet over low heat until lightly browned, stirring occasionally.

Spice Things Up

- Onion & Green Chile Enchiladas
- Eddie's Favorite Fiesta Corn
- Spicy Pork & Green Chili Verde
- Agua de Jamaica

ONION & GREEN CHILE ENCHILADAS

My family lobbies for my famous enchiladas. I usually make a meatless version, but feel free to add cooked chicken.

—Anthony Bolton, Bellevue, NE

PREP: 20 MIN. • **BAKE:** 20 MIN. • **MAKES:** 6 SERVINGS

- **2 Tbsp. butter**
- **3 large onions, sliced (about 6 cups)**
- **2 cups shredded cheddar cheese, divided**
- **1 cup sour cream**
- **⅓ cup salsa**
- **2 Tbsp. reduced-sodium taco seasoning**
- **12 flour tortillas (6 in.)**
- **2 cans (10 oz. each) green enchilada sauce**
- **Minced fresh cilantro, optional**

1. Preheat oven to 350°. In a large skillet, heat butter over medium heat. Add onions; cook and stir under tender and golden brown, 8-10 minutes. Cool slightly.

2. Meanwhile, in a large bowl, combine 1 cup cheese, sour cream, salsa and taco seasoning. Stir in cooled onions.

3. Place 2 Tbsp. mixture off center on each tortilla. Roll up and place in a well-greased 13x9-in. baking dish, seam side down. Top with sauce; sprinkle with remaining cheese.

4. Bake, uncovered, until enchiladas are heated through and cheese is melted, 20-25 minutes. Sprinkle with minced cilantro, if desired.

2 ENCHILADAS: 561 cal., 32g fat (18g sat. fat), 76mg chol., 1466mg sod., 50g carb. (9g sugars, 4g fiber), 17g pro.

EDDIE'S FAVORITE FIESTA CORN

When sweet corn is available, I love making this splurge of a side dish. Frozen corn works, but taste as you go and add sugar if needed.

—Anthony Bolton, Bellevue, NE

PREP: 15 MIN. • **COOK:** 25 MIN. • **MAKES:** 8 SERVINGS

- **½ lb. bacon strips, chopped**
- **5 cups fresh or frozen super sweet corn**
- **1 medium sweet red pepper, finely chopped**
- **1 medium sweet yellow pepper, finely chopped**
- **1 pkg. (8 oz.) reduced-fat cream cheese**
- **½ cup half-and-half cream**
- **1 can (4 oz.) chopped green chiles, optional**
- **2 tsp. sugar**
- **1 tsp. pepper**
- **¼ tsp. salt**

1. In a 6-qt. stockpot, cook bacon over medium heat until crisp, stirring occasionally. Remove with a slotted spoon; drain on paper towels. Discard drippings, reserving 1 Tbsp. in pan.

2. Add corn, red pepper and yellow pepper to drippings; cook and stir over medium-high heat 5-6 minutes or until tender. Stir in remaining ingredients until blended; bring to a boil. Reduce heat; simmer, covered, 8-10 minutes or until thickened.

⅔ CUP: 249 cal., 14g fat (7g sat. fat), 39mg chol., 399mg sod., 22g carb. (9g sugars, 2g fiber), 10g pro.

SPICY PORK & GREEN CHILI VERDE

My pork chili is brimming with poblano and sweet red peppers for a hearty kick. Serve it with sour cream, Monterey Jack and tortilla chips.

—Anthony Bolton, Bellevue, NE

PREP: 40 MIN. + STANDING • **COOK:** 25 MIN. • **MAKES:** 6 SERVINGS

- **6 poblano peppers**
- **2 Tbsp. butter**
- **1½ lbs. pork tenderloin, cut into 1-in. pieces**
- **2 medium sweet red or yellow peppers, coarsely chopped**
- **1 large sweet onion, coarsely chopped**
- **1 jalapeno pepper, seeded and finely chopped**
- **2 Tbsp. chili powder**
- **2 garlic cloves, minced**
- **1 tsp. salt**
- **¼ tsp. ground nutmeg**
- **2 cups chicken broth**
- **Optional toppings: Sour cream, shredded Monterey Jack cheese, crumbled tortilla chips and lime wedges**

1. Place poblano peppers on a foil-lined baking sheet. Broil 4 in. from heat until skins blister, about 5 minutes. With tongs, rotate the peppers a quarter turn. Broil and rotate until all sides are blistered and blackened. Immediately place peppers in a large bowl; let stand, covered, 10 minutes.

2. Peel off and discard charred skin. Remove and discard stems and seeds. Finely chop peppers.

3. In a 6-qt. stockpot, heat butter over medium heat. Brown pork in batches. Remove with a slotted spoon.

4. In same pan, add red peppers, onion and jalapeno; cook, covered, over medium heat 8-10 minutes or until tender, stirring occasionally. Stir in chili powder, garlic, salt and nutmeg. Add broth, roasted peppers and pork; bring to a boil. Reduce heat; simmer, uncovered, 10-15 minutes or until pork is tender. Serve with toppings as desired.

1 CUP: 235 cal., 9g fat (4g sat. fat), 75mg chol., 913mg sod., 14g carb. (8g sugars, 4g fiber), 25g pro.

AGUA DE JAMAICA

This is an iced tea made from hibiscus. I love the deep color and how it goes with just about any meal. Feel free to leave out the rum if you'd like.

—Adan Franco, Milwaukee, WI

PREP: 15 MIN. + CHILLING • **MAKES:** 6 SERVINGS

- **1 cup dried hibiscus flowers or 6 hibiscus tea bags**
- **5 cups water, divided**
- **1½ tsp. grated lime zest**
- **½ cup sugar**
- **1 cup rum, optional**
- **Mint sprigs, optional**

1. Rinse flowers in cold water. In a large saucepan, combine 3 cups water, flowers and lime zest. Bring to a boil. Reduce heat; simmer, uncovered, 10 minutes.

2. Remove from heat; let stand 15 minutes. Strain mixture, discarding flowers and zest; transfer to a large bowl. Add sugar and remaining water, stirring until sugar is dissolved. If desired, stir in rum. Refrigerate until cold. Add mint sprigs if desired.

¾ CUP: 67 cal., 0 fat (0 sat. fat), 0 chol., 2mg sod., 17g carb. (17g sugars, 0 fiber), 0 pro.

FAMILY FIESTA

It's Sunday afternoon, and the comforting aroma of beans and rice wafts through Delfina Delgadillo's bustling home. Each week, her big family comes together around faith and a home-cooked Mexican meal.

Young grandkids bound through the living room; cousins set the table; and aunts tote spicy chicken, cookies and tortillas to the kitchen to prepare for the come-as-you-are feast. Every week, nearly 20 people pop by Grandma's house, including the newest family member, Missy Franco. Missy and her husband, Adan, married a few years ago, but she knew how close-knit his family was from the start. "The first time I met Adan's family was at a summer party for their grandma. Imagine being introduced to more than 75 people in one sitting!" Missy says, laughing. "It was intimidating and wonderful all at once."

Adan's grandparents came to Wisconsin from Mexico, and as the family grew, the dinners became a touchstone. "My family gathers every Sunday afternoon for a meal," Adan says. "Birthdays blend with holidays and turn into picnics and parties." Adan says that chicken tacos are menu staples. "Chicken is a no-brainer when it comes to mealtime—from weekday suppers to special weekend meals."

Adan, a professional chef, credits these meals for more than the delicious food. "Not only do I believe in sharing weeknight meals with immediate family, but my appreciation for cooking came from watching my mother and grandmother cook," he says. "Endless support—and rice—keep our family tradition alive every week!"

Adan and Missy Franco (at head of table) enjoy meals spent with Grandma Delfina (at left) and extended family.

A Sunday Roast
• Thyme & Basil Roast Pork
• Honey-Lemon Asparagus
• Parmesan Baked Potatoes
• Raspberry Rumble

THYME & BASIL ROAST PORK

Dad's favorite roast pork was rubbed with cinnamon, thyme, basil and lemon. He loved thick, juicy slices. Try the leftovers on sandwiches.

—Lorraine Caland, Shuniah, ON

PREP: 30 MIN. • **BAKE:** 1 HOUR + STANDING • **MAKES:** 8 SERVINGS

- **1 Tbsp. all-purpose flour**
- **2 tsp. dried basil**
- **2 tsp. dried thyme**
- **2 tsp. ground cinnamon**
- **1½ tsp. salt**
- **½ tsp. pepper**
- **1 boneless pork loin roast (3 to 4 lbs.)**
- **2 Tbsp. canola oil**
- **1 medium apple, cut into wedges**
- **1 medium onion, cut into wedges**
- **1 medium lemon, cut into wedges**
- **1 fresh rosemary sprig**

1. Preheat oven to 325°. In a small bowl, mix flour, basil, thyme, cinnamon, salt and pepper; rub over pork.

2. In a large skillet, heat oil over medium-high heat. Brown roast on all sides. Place roast in a shallow roasting pan, fat side up. Arrange apple and onion around roast. Squeeze lemon juice from 1 wedge over pork; add lemon wedges to pan. Place rosemary over pork.

3. Roast 1-1½ hours or until a thermometer reads 145°. Remove roast, onion and apple to a serving platter; tent with foil. Let stand 15 minutes before slicing.

4 OZ. COOKED PORK: 266 cal., 11g fat (3g sat. fat), 85mg chol., 493mg sod., 6g carb. (3g sugars, 1g fiber), 33g pro.

DIABETIC EXCHANGES: 4 lean meat, 1 fat, ½ starch.

HONEY-LEMON ASPARAGUS

Everyone who tastes my glazed asparagus takes a second helping, so I usually double the recipe. For another option, try using a root vegetable like turnip or parsnip.

—Lorraine Caland, Shuniah, ON

TAKES: 15 MIN. • **MAKES:** 8 SERVINGS

- **2 lbs. fresh asparagus, trimmed**
- **¼ cup honey**
- **2 Tbsp. butter**
- **2 Tbsp. lemon juice**
- **1 tsp. sea salt**
- **1 tsp. balsamic vinegar**
- **1 tsp. Worcestershire sauce**
- **Additional sea salt, optional**

1. In a large saucepan, bring 8 cups water to a boil. Add the asparagus in batches; cook, uncovered, 1-2 minutes or just until crisp-tender. Drain and pat dry.

2. Meanwhile, in a small saucepan, combine the remaining ingredients. Bring to a boil. Reduce heat; simmer, uncovered, 2 minutes or until slightly thickened.

3. Transfer asparagus to a large bowl; drizzle with glaze and toss gently to coat. If desired, sprinkle with additional sea salt.

1 SERVING: 73 cal., 3g fat (2g sat. fat), 8mg chol., 276mg sod., 12g carb. (10g sugars, 1g fiber), 2g pro.

DIABETIC EXCHANGES: 1 vegetable, ½ starch, ½ fat.

PARMESAN BAKED POTATOES

Who knew a simple recipe could make potatoes taste so good? Mom liked to make them for special dinners because they were better than ordinary baked potatoes.

—Ruth Seitz, Columbus Junction, IA

PREP: 5 MIN. • **BAKE:** 40 MIN. • **MAKES:** 8 SERVINGS

- **6 Tbsp. butter, melted**
- **3 Tbsp. grated Parmesan cheese**
- **8 medium unpeeled red potatoes (about 2¾ lbs.), halved lengthwise**

Pour butter into a 13x9-in. baking pan. Sprinkle Parmesan cheese over butter. Place the potatoes with cut sides down over cheese. Bake, uncovered, at 400° for 40-45 minutes or until tender.

2 POTATO HALVES: 165 cal., 9g fat (6g sat. fat), 24mg chol., 128mg sod., 18g carb. (1g sugars, 2g fiber), 3g pro.

RASPBERRY RUMBLE

My guy is a raspberry fan, so that's what I use in this cake with a classic fluffy frosting. I freeze the berries so they don't stain the batter.

—Lorraine Caland, Shuniah, ON

PREP: 40 MIN. • **BAKE:** 25 MIN. + COOLING • **MAKES:** 12 SERVINGS

- **2 cups fresh raspberries**
- **¼ cup butter, softened**
- **¾ cup sugar**
- **2 large eggs, room temperature**
- **2¼ cups all-purpose flour**
- **2 tsp. baking powder**
- **1 tsp. salt**
- **¾ cup 2% milk**

TOPPING

- **3 large egg whites**
- **1 cup sugar**
- **⅛ tsp. cream of tartar**
- **¼ to ½ cup boiling water, optional**
- **¼ tsp. almond extract**
- **Sliced almonds**

1. Place raspberries on a baking sheet; freeze until firm. Preheat oven to 350°.

2. In a large bowl, cream butter and sugar until light and fluffy, 5-7 minutes; beat in eggs. In another bowl, whisk together flour, baking powder and salt; add to creamed mixture alternately with milk, beating well. Fold in frozen raspberries. Spread into a greased 13x9-in. baking pan.

3. Bake 25-30 minutes or until a toothpick inserted in center comes out clean. Cool completely in pan on a wire rack.

4. For topping, whisk together egg whites, sugar and cream of tartar in a large heatproof bowl. Place over simmering water in a large saucepan over medium heat; whisking constantly, heat mixture until a thermometer reads 160°. Remove from heat.

5. Beat on high speed until stiff glossy peaks form, about 5 minutes. If desired, thin the frosting by slowly beating in enough boiling water to reach desired consistency. Fold in almond extract. Spread over cake. Sprinkle with almonds. Refrigerate leftovers.

1 PIECE: 266 cal., 5g fat (3g sat. fat), 42mg chol., 323mg sod., 51g carb. (31g sugars, 2g fiber), 5g pro.

A New Take on Meatloaf

- Tex-Mex Meat Loaf
- Spanish Rice
- Sweet Buttery Cornbread
- Shortcut Tres Leches Cake

TEX-MEX MEAT LOAF

Here's a zesty, flavorful meat loaf you can really sink your teeth into. Best of all, it's made in a slow cooker! Serve it with Spanish rice and cornbread, or simply enjoy it alongside black beans and a green salad.

—Kristen Miller, Glendale, WI

PREP: 25 MIN. • **COOK:** 3 HOURS + STANDING • **MAKES:** 1 LOAF (6 SERVINGS)

- **2 slices white bread, torn into small pieces**
- **⅓ cup 2% milk**
- **1 lb. lean ground turkey**
- **½ lb. fresh chorizo**
- **1 medium sweet red pepper, finely chopped**
- **1 small onion, finely chopped**
- **1 jalapeno pepper, seeded and finely chopped**
- **2 large eggs, lightly beaten**
- **2 Tbsp. minced fresh cilantro**
- **2 garlic cloves, minced**
- **2 tsp. chili powder**
- **1 tsp. salt**
- **1 tsp. ground cumin**
- **½ tsp. dried oregano**
- **½ tsp. pepper**
- **¼ tsp. cayenne pepper**
- **⅔ cup salsa, divided**
- **Additional minced fresh cilantro**

1. Combine bread and milk in a large bowl; let stand until liquid is absorbed. Add next 14 ingredients and ⅓ cup salsa; mix lightly but thoroughly.

2. On an 18x7-in. piece of heavy-duty foil, shape meat mixture into a 10x6-in. oval loaf. Lifting with foil, transfer to a 6-qt. oval slow cooker. Press ends of foil up sides of slow cooker.

3. Cook, covered, on low 3-4 hours or until a thermometer reads 165°. Lifting with foil, drain fat into slow cooker before removing meat loaf to a platter; top with remaining salsa and sprinkle with cilantro. Let stand 10 minutes before slicing.

1 SLICE: 335 cal., 20g fat (6g sat. fat), 149mg chol., 1109mg sod., 11g carb. (4g sugars, 1g fiber), 27g pro.

SPANISH RICE

You'll find my Spanish rice is so much better than any boxed variety in grocery stores. And it can be prepared in about the same time as those convenience foods, using items found in your pantry. Garnish with cilantro for extra flair!

—Anne Yaeger, Washington, DC

TAKES: 25 MIN. • **MAKES:** 6 SERVINGS

- **¼ cup butter, cubed**
- **2 cups uncooked instant rice**
- **1 can (14½ oz.) diced tomatoes, undrained**
- **1 cup boiling water**
- **2 beef bouillon cubes**
- **1 medium onion, chopped**
- **1 garlic clove, minced**
- **1 bay leaf**
- **1 tsp. sugar**
- **1 tsp. salt**
- **¼ tsp. pepper**

In a saucepan, melt butter over medium heat. Add rice; cook and stir until lightly browned. Add remaining ingredients; bring to a boil. Reduce heat; cover and simmer until the liquid is absorbed and rice is tender, 10-15 minutes. Remove bay leaf before serving.

¾ CUP: 217 cal., 8g fat (5g sat. fat), 20mg chol., 886mg sod., 33g carb. (4g sugars, 2g fiber), 4g pro.

OPINEL

SWEET BUTTERY CORNBREAD

A friend gave me this cornbread recipe several years ago, and it's my favorite of all I've tried. I love to serve the melt-in-your mouth cornbread hot from the oven with butter and syrup. It always gets rave reviews.

—Nicole Callen, Auburn, California

PREP: 15 MIN. • **BAKE:** 10 MIN. • **MAKES:** 15 SERVINGS

- **⅔ cup butter, softened**
- **1 cup sugar**
- **3 large eggs, room temperature**
- **1⅔ cups 2% milk**
- **2⅓ cups all-purpose flour**
- **1 cup cornmeal**
- **4½ teaspoons baking powder**
- **1 teaspoon salt**

1. Preheat oven to 400°. In a large bowl, cream butter and sugar until light and fluffy, 5-7 minutes. Combine eggs and milk. Combine flour, cornmeal, baking powder and salt; add to creamed mixture alternately with egg mixture.

2. Pour into a greased 13x9-in. baking pan. Bake 22-27 minutes or until a toothpick inserted in center comes out clean. Cut into squares; serve warm.

1 PIECE: 259 cal., 10g fat (6g sat. fat), 68mg chol., 386mg sod., 37g carb. (15g sugars, 1g fiber), 5g pro.

SHORTCUT TRES LECHES CAKE

My mom's favorite cake is tres leches, a butter cake soaked in three kinds of milk. I developed a no-fuss version that's rich and tender.

—Marina Castle Kelley, Canyon Country, CA

PREP: 20 MIN. + CHILLING • **BAKE:** 30 MIN. + COOLING • **MAKES:** 20 SERVINGS

- **1 pkg. butter recipe golden cake or yellow cake mix (regular size)**
- **3 large eggs, room temperature**
- **⅔ cup 2% milk**
- **½ cup butter, softened**
- **1 tsp. vanilla extract**

TOPPING

- **1 can (14 oz.) sweetened condensed milk**
- **1 can (12 oz.) evaporated milk**
- **1 cup heavy whipping cream**

WHIPPED CREAM

- **1 cup heavy whipping cream**
- **3 Tbsp. confectioners' sugar**
- **1 tsp. vanilla extract**

1. Preheat oven to 350°. Grease a 13x9-in. baking pan.

2. In a large bowl, combine cake mix, eggs, milk, softened butter and vanilla; beat on low speed 30 seconds. Beat on medium for 2 minutes. Transfer to prepared pan. Bake 30-35 minutes or until a toothpick inserted in center comes out clean. Cool in pan on a wire rack 20 minutes.

3. In a 4-cup measuring cup, whisk the topping ingredients until blended. Using a skewer, generously poke holes in top of warm cake. Pour milk mixture slowly over cake, filling holes. Cool 30 minutes longer. Refrigerate, covered, at least 4 hours or overnight.

4. In a bowl, beat cream until it begins to thicken. Add the confectioners' sugar and vanilla; beat until soft peaks form. Spread over cake.

1 PIECE: 343 cal., 20g fat (12g sat. fat), 89mg chol., 257mg sod., 36g carb. (28g sugars, 0 fiber), 6g pro.

Classic Roast Beef Dinner

- Peppery Roast Beef
- Roasted Red Pepper Green Beans
- Raw Cauliflower Tabbouleh
- Biltmore's Bread Pudding

PEPPERY ROAST BEEF

With its spicy coating and creamy horseradish sauce, this tender roast will be the star of any dinner. My family and friends love it—and it's so simple to make.

—Maureen Brand, Somers, IA

PREP: 15 MIN. • **BAKE:** 2½ HOURS + STANDING • **MAKES:** 12 SERVINGS

1 Tbsp. olive oil
1 Tbsp. seasoned pepper
2 garlic cloves, minced
½ tsp. dried thyme
¼ tsp. salt
1 boneless beef eye round or top round roast (4 to 5 lbs.)

HORSERADISH SAUCE

1 cup sour cream
2 Tbsp. lemon juice
2 Tbsp. milk
2 Tbsp. prepared horseradish
1 Tbsp. Dijon mustard
¼ tsp. salt
⅛ tsp. pepper

1. Preheat oven to 325°. In a small bowl, combine the oil, seasoned pepper, garlic, thyme and salt; rub over roast. Place fat side up on a rack in a shallow roasting pan.

2. Bake, uncovered, 2½-3 hours or until meat reaches desired doneness (for medium-rare, a thermometer should read 135°; medium, 140°; medium-well, 145°). Let stand for 10 minutes before slicing.

3. In a bowl, combine the sauce ingredients. Serve with roast.

4 OZ. COOKED BEEF WITH ABOUT 1 TBSP. SAUCE: 228 cal., 10g fat (4g sat. fat), 83mg chol., 211mg sod., 3g carb. (1g sugars, 0 fiber), 30g pro.

ROASTED RED PEPPER GREEN BEANS

This recipe showcases a creamy sauce with shallot-and-chive cheese. The toasted pine nuts add crunch. Just a few ingredients—so easy!

—Becky Ellis, Roanoke, VA

TAKES: 20 MIN. • **MAKES:** 10 SERVINGS

- **2 lbs. fresh green beans, trimmed**
- **1 Tbsp. butter**
- **½ cup pine nuts**
- **Dash salt**
- **1 pkg. (5.2 oz.) shallot-chive spreadable cheese**
- **1 jar (8 oz.) roasted sweet red peppers, drained and chopped**

1. In a pot of boiling water, cook green beans until tender, about 6-8 minutes.

2. Meanwhile, in a large skillet, melt butter over medium heat. Add pine nuts; cook and stir until lightly browned, 3-4 minutes. Remove from heat; sprinkle with salt.

3. Drain beans; return to pot. Place cheese over warm beans to soften; toss to coat. Add red peppers; toss to combine. Sprinkle with pine nuts. Serve immediately.

¾ CUP: 152 cal., 12g fat (5g sat. fat), 18mg chol., 341mg sod., 9g carb. (3g sugars, 3g fiber), 4g pro.

RAW CAULIFLOWER TABBOULEH

This recipe comes together quickly. I love that I can serve it to nearly anyone at my table with special dietary restrictions.

—Maiah Miller, Montclair, VA

PREP: 10 MIN. + CHILLING • **MAKES:** 6 CUPS

- **1 medium head cauliflower**
- **½ cup oil-packed sun-dried tomatoes**
- **12 pitted Greek olives**
- **2 cups fresh parsley leaves**
- **1 cup fresh cilantro leaves**
- **1 Tbsp. white wine vinegar or cider vinegar**
- **¼ tsp. salt**
- **¼ tsp. pepper**

Core and coarsely chop cauliflower. In batches, pulse cauliflower in a food processor until it resembles rice (do not overprocess). Transfer to a large bowl. Add remaining ingredients to food processor; pulse until finely chopped. Add to cauliflower; toss to combine. Refrigerate 1 hour before serving to allow flavors to blend.

¾ CUP: 55 cal., 3g fat (0 sat. fat), 0 chol., 215mg sod., 7g carb. (2g sugars, 2g fiber), 2g pro.

BILTMORE'S BREAD PUDDING

Here's one of our classic dessert recipes. A golden caramel sauce enhances the rich bread pudding.

—Biltmore Estate, Asheville, NC

PREP: 30 MIN. • **BAKE:** 40 MIN. • **MAKES:** 12 SERVINGS

- **8 cups cubed day-old bread**
- **9 large eggs, room temperature**
- **2¼ cups 2% milk**
- **1¾ cups heavy whipping cream**
- **1 cup sugar**
- **¾ cup butter, melted**
- **3 tsp. vanilla extract**
- **1½ tsp. ground cinnamon**

CARAMEL SAUCE

- **1 cup sugar**
- **¼ cup water**
- **1 Tbsp. lemon juice**
- **2 Tbsp. butter**
- **1 cup heavy whipping cream**

1. Place bread cubes in a greased 13x9-in. baking dish. In a large bowl, whisk the eggs, milk, cream, sugar, butter, vanilla and cinnamon. Pour evenly over bread.

2. Bake, uncovered, at 350° for 40-45 minutes or until a knife inserted in the center comes out clean. Let stand for 5 minutes before cutting.

3. Meanwhile, in a small saucepan, bring the sugar, water and lemon juice to a boil. Reduce heat to medium; cook until sugar is dissolved and mixture turns a golden amber color. Stir in butter until melted. Gradually stir in cream. Serve with bread pudding.

1 PIECE WITH ABOUT 2 TBSP. SAUCE: 581 cal., 39g fat (23g sat. fat), 273mg chol., 345mg sod., 49g carb. (37g sugars, 1g fiber), 9g pro.

Roast Chicken Made Easy
• Slow-Cooker Roast Chicken
• Fresh Sugar Snap Pea Salad
• Scalloped Potatoes with Mushrooms
• Lemon Curd-Filled Angel Food Cake

SLOW-COOKER ROAST CHICKEN

This chicken dinner is so easy to make in a slow cooker. We shred the leftovers, and use the chicken in meals throughout the week.

—Courtney Stultz, Weir, KS

PREP: 20 MIN. • **COOK:** 4 HOURS + STANDING • **MAKES:** 6 SERVINGS

- **2 medium carrots, cut into 1-in. pieces**
- **1 medium onion, cut into 1-in. pieces**
- **2 garlic cloves, minced**
- **2 tsp. olive oil**
- **1 tsp. dried parsley flakes**
- **1 tsp. pepper**
- **¾ tsp. salt**
- **½ tsp. dried oregano**
- **½ tsp. rubbed sage**
- **½ tsp. chili powder**
- **1 broiler/fryer chicken (4 to 5 lbs.)**

1. Place carrots and onion in a 6-qt. slow cooker. In a small bowl, mix garlic and oil. In another bowl, mix dry seasonings.

2. Tuck wings under chicken; tie drumsticks together. With fingers, carefully loosen skin from chicken breast; rub garlic mixture under the skin. Secure skin to underside of the breast with toothpicks.

3. Place chicken in slow cooker over carrots and onions, breast side up; sprinkle with seasoning mixture. Cook, covered, on low 4-5 hours, or until a thermometer inserted in thigh reads at least 170°.

4. Remove chicken from slow cooker; tent with foil. Discard vegetables. Let chicken stand 15 minutes before carving.

FREEZE OPTION: Cool chicken pieces and any juices. Freeze in freezer containers. To use, partially thaw in refrigerator overnight. Heat through slowly in a covered skillet until a thermometer inserted in the chicken reads 165°, stirring occasionally and adding a little broth or water if necessary.

5 OZ. COOKED CHICKEN: 408 cal., 24g fat (6g sat. fat), 139mg chol., 422mg sod., 1g carb. (0 sugars, 0 fiber), 44g pro.

FRESH SUGAR SNAP PEA SALAD

We found fresh sugar snap peas at the local produce market, and discovered they make a cheerful salad with a quick and tasty onion dressing.

—Courtney Stultz, Weir, KS

PREP: 15 MIN. + CHILLING • **MAKES:** 6 SERVINGS

- **2 Tbsp. olive oil**
- **2 Tbsp. white wine vinegar**
- **2 tsp. honey**
- **½ tsp. salt**
- **½ tsp. pepper**
- **¼ tsp. dried thyme**
- **½ cup chopped onion**
- **½ tsp. poppy seeds**
- **1 lb. fresh sugar snap peas, trimmed and halved (about 4 cups)**

1. Place the first 7 ingredients in a blender; cover and process until blended. Transfer to a large bowl; stir in poppy seeds.

2. Add peas to dressing and toss to coat. Refrigerate, covered, 30 minutes before serving.

⅔ CUP: 86 cal., 5g fat (1g sat. fat), 0 chol., 201mg sod., 9g carb. (5g sugars, 2g fiber), 3g pro.

DIABETIC EXCHANGES: 1 vegetable, 1 fat.

SCALLOPED POTATOES WITH MUSHROOMS

Potatoes and mushrooms make a one-dish meal I absolutely love. Give it a try and you'll see what I mean!

—Courtney Stultz, Weir, KS

PREP: 40 MIN. • **BAKE:** 15 MIN. + STANDING • **MAKES:** 8 SERVINGS

- **2 lbs. potatoes (about 4 medium), peeled and sliced**
- **1 Tbsp. butter**
- **½ lb. sliced fresh mushrooms**
- **1 small onion, chopped**
- **1 garlic clove, minced**
- **¼ cup all-purpose flour**
- **1 cup chicken broth**
- **1 tsp. salt**
- **½ tsp. dried oregano**
- **½ tsp. pepper**
- **1 cup sour cream**
- **1 cup coarsely chopped fresh spinach**
- **2 cups shredded Swiss cheese**

1. Preheat oven to 375°. Place potatoes in a large saucepan; add water to cover. Bring to a boil. Reduce heat; cook, uncovered, until tender, 8-12 minutes. Drain.

2. Meanwhile, in another saucepan, heat butter over medium-high heat. Add mushrooms and onion; cook and stir 6-8 minutes or until tender. Stir in garlic; cook 1 minute longer.

3. In a small bowl, whisk flour, broth and seasonings until smooth; stir into mushroom mixture. Bring to a boil, stirring constantly; cook and stir until sauce is thickened, 1-2 minutes. Remove from heat; stir in sour cream.

4. Arrange half of the potatoes in a greased 1½-qt. or 8-in. square baking dish; top with spinach. Spread half of the hot mushroom sauce over top; sprinkle with 1 cup cheese. Layer with remaining potatoes, sauce and cheese.

5. Bake, uncovered, until heated through and cheese is melted, 12-15 minutes. Let stand 10 minutes before serving.

1 CUP: 269 cal., 14g fat (9g sat. fat), 49mg chol., 471mg sod., 23g carb. (4g sugars, 2g fiber), 11g pro.

LEMON CURD-FILLED ANGEL FOOD CAKE

For a sunny angel food cake, we make a filling of mascarpone, cream cheese and lemon curd, and then drizzle the cake with a lemony sweet glaze.

—Leah Rekau, Milwaukee, WI

PREP: 55 MIN. + CHILLING • **BAKE:** 45 MIN. + COOLING • **MAKES:** 16 SERVINGS

- **12 large egg whites (about 1⅔ cups)**
- **1 cup cake flour**
- **1½ cups sugar, divided**
- **1 vanilla bean or 1 tsp. vanilla extract**
- **½ tsp. cream of tartar**
- **¼ tsp. salt**

FILLING

- **½ cup heavy whipping cream**
- **½ cup mascarpone cheese**
- **2 Tbsp. confectioners' sugar**
- **1 jar (10 oz.) lemon curd, divided**
- **1 cup sliced fresh strawberries, patted dry**

GLAZE

- **2 cups confectioners' sugar**
- **1 tsp. grated lemon zest**
- **3 to 4 Tbsp. lemon juice**

1. Place egg whites in a large bowl; let stand at room temperature 30 minutes.

2. Preheat oven to 325°. In a small bowl, mix flour and ¾ cup sugar until blended.

3. Add seeds from vanilla bean (or extract if using), cream of tartar and salt to egg whites. Beat on medium speed until soft peaks form. Gradually add remaining ¾ cup sugar, 1 Tbsp. at a time, beating on high after each addition until sugar is dissolved. Continue beating until soft glossy peaks form. Gradually fold in flour mixture, about ½ cup at a time.

4. Gently transfer batter to an ungreased 10-in. tube pan. Cut through batter with a knife to remove air pockets. Bake on lowest oven rack 45-55 minutes or until top springs back when lightly touched. Immediately invert pan; cool completely in pan, about 1½ hours.

5. Run a knife around sides and center tube of pan. Remove cake to a serving plate. Using a serrated knife, cut a 1-in. slice off top of cake. Hollow out remaining cake, leaving a 1-in.-thick shell (save removed cake for another use).

6. For filling, in a small bowl, beat cream until it begins to thicken. Add mascarpone cheese and confectioners' sugar; beat until soft peaks form. Fold in ¼ cup of the lemon curd.

7. Line bottom of tunnel with strawberries. Spoon mascarpone mixture over berries; top with remaining lemon curd. Replace cake top; refrigerate, covered, at least 4 hours or overnight.

8. For glaze, in a small bowl, mix confectioners' sugar, lemon zest and enough juice to reach desired consistency. Unwrap cake; spread glaze over top, allowing some to drip down sides. Refrigerate until serving.

1 SLICE: 315 cal., 10g fat (6g sat. fat), 41mg chol., 91mg sod., 52g carb. (44g sugars, 0 fiber), 4g pro.

Old-World Flavor
• Pork Shepherd's Pie
• Garlic-Herb Pattypan Squash
• Old-World Rye Bread
• Butternut Harvest Pies

PORK SHEPHERD'S PIE

Of all the shepherd's pie recipes I've tried through the years, this one is definitely the best. I enjoy cooking for my family, and everyone agrees this meaty pie is a keeper.

—Mary Arthurs, Etobicoke, ON

PREP: 30 MIN. • **BAKE:** 45 MIN. • **MAKES:** 6 SERVINGS

PORK LAYER

- **1 lb. ground pork**
- **1 small onion, chopped**
- **2 garlic cloves, minced**
- **1 cup cooked rice**
- **½ cup pork gravy or ¼ cup chicken broth**
- **½ tsp. salt**
- **½ tsp. dried thyme**

CABBAGE LAYER

- **1 medium carrot, diced**
- **1 small onion, chopped**
- **2 Tbsp. butter or margarine**
- **6 cups chopped cabbage**
- **1 cup chicken broth**
- **½ tsp. salt**
- **¼ tsp. pepper**

POTATO LAYER

- **2 cups mashed potatoes**
- **¼ cup shredded cheddar cheese**

1. In a skillet over medium heat, brown pork until no longer pink. Add onion and garlic. Cook until vegetables are tender; drain. Stir in rice, gravy, salt and thyme. Spoon into a greased 11x7-in. baking dish.

2. In the same skillet, saute carrot and onion in butter over medium heat for 5 minutes. Stir in cabbage; cook for about 1 minute. Add the broth, salt and pepper; cover and cook for 10 minutes. Spoon over pork layer.

3. Spoon or pipe mashed potatoes on top; sprinkle with cheese. Bake, uncovered, at 350° for 45 minutes or until browned.

1 CUP: 365 cal., 19g fat (8g sat. fat), 66mg chol., 1045mg sod., 28g carb. (5g sugars, 4g fiber), 19g pro.

GARLIC-HERB PATTYPAN SQUASH

The first time I grew a garden, I harvested summer squash and cooked it with garlic and herbs. I quickly found that using pattypan squash works beautifully, too.

—Kaycee Mason, Siloam Spgs, AR

TAKES: 25 MIN. • **MAKES:** 4 SERVINGS

- **5 cups halved small pattypan squash (about 1¼ lbs.)**
- **1 Tbsp. olive oil**
- **2 garlic cloves, minced**
- **½ tsp. salt**
- **¼ tsp. dried oregano**
- **¼ tsp. dried thyme**
- **¼ tsp. pepper**
- **1 Tbsp. minced fresh parsley**

Preheat oven to 425°. Place squash in a greased 15x10x1-in. baking pan. Mix oil, garlic, salt, oregano, thyme and pepper; drizzle over squash. Toss to coat. Roast 15-20 minutes or until tender, stirring occasionally. Sprinkle with parsley.

⅔ CUP: 58 cal., 3g fat (0 sat. fat), 0 chol., 296mg sod., 6g carb. (3g sugars, 2g fiber), 2g pro.

DIABETIC EXCHANGES: 1 vegetable, ½ fat.

OLD-WORLD RYE BREAD

Rye and caraway give this bread wonderful flavor, while the surprise ingredient of baking cocoa adds to the rich, dark color. I sometimes stir in a cup each of raisins and walnuts.

—Perlene Hoekema, Lynden, WA

PREP: 25 MIN. + RISING • **BAKE:** 35 MIN. + COOLING • **MAKES:** 2 LOAVES (12 SLICES EACH)

- **2 pkg. (¼ oz. each) active dry yeast**
- **1½ cups warm water (110° to 115°)**
- **½ cup molasses**
- **6 Tbsp. butter, softened**
- **2 cups rye flour**
- **¼ cup baking cocoa**
- **2 Tbsp. caraway seeds**
- **2 tsp. salt**
- **3½ to 4 cups all-purpose flour**
- **Cornmeal**

1. In a large bowl, dissolve yeast in warm water. Beat in the molasses, butter, rye flour, cocoa, caraway seeds, salt and 2 cups all-purpose flour until smooth. Stir in enough of the remaining all-purpose flour to form a stiff dough.

2. Turn onto a floured surface; knead until smooth and elastic, 6-8 minutes. Place in a greased bowl, turning once to grease top. Cover and let rise in a warm place until doubled, about 1½ hours.

3. Punch dough down. Turn onto a lightly floured surface; divide in half. Shape each piece into a loaf about 10 in. long. Grease 2 baking sheets and sprinkle with cornmeal. Place loaves on prepared pans. Cover and let rise until doubled, about 1 hour.

4. Bake at 350° for 35-40 minutes or until bread sounds hollow when tapped. Remove from pans to wire racks to cool.

1 PIECE: 146 cal., 3g fat (2g sat. fat), 8mg chol., 229mg sod., 26g carb. (5g sugars, 2g fiber), 3g pro.

BUTTERNUT HARVEST PIES

This egg- and dairy-free pie is a great alternative to standard pumpkin pie! We love to make the pies with squash from our garden. Feel free to amp up the flavor even further by adding more of your favorite spices. You'll be glad the recipe makes two.

—Juliana Thetford, Ellwood City, PA

PREP: 65 MIN. • **BAKE:** 40 MIN. + CHILLING • **MAKES:** 2 PIES (6 SERVINGS EACH)

- **1 large butternut squash (about 4 lbs.)**
- **1 pkg. (10½ oz.) silken firm tofu**
- **1 cup sugar**
- **⅓ cup cornstarch**
- **2 Tbsp. honey**
- **2 tsp. ground cinnamon**
- **1 tsp. ground ginger**
- **1 tsp. ground nutmeg or ground mace**
- **2 graham cracker crusts (9 in.)**
- **Sweetened whipped cream, optional**

1. Preheat oven to 400°. Halve squash lengthwise; discard seeds. Place squash on a baking sheet, cut side down. Roast until tender, 45-55 minutes. Cool slightly. Scoop out pulp and mash (you should have about 4 cups).

2. Place tofu, sugar, cornstarch, honey and spices in a food processor; process until smooth. Add squash; pulse just until blended. Divide between crusts.

3. Bake at 400° until a knife inserted in the center comes out clean, 40-50 minutes. Cool 1 hour on a wire rack. Refrigerate, covered, until cold. If desired, serve with whipped cream.

1 PIECE: 281 cal., 8g fat (2g sat. fat), 0 chol., 174mg sod., 51g carb. (35g sugars, 3g fiber), 4g pro.

Taste of Italy
• Sausage Lasagna
• Risotto Balls (Arancini)
• Italian Pinwheel Rolls
• Italian Cream Cheese Cake

SAUSAGE LASAGNA

The idea for this sausage lasagna recipe comes from my mother-in-law, who always makes it for my three boys. I've put an easy twist on Carole's classic dish, and it's become one of my go-to dinners as well.

—Blair Lonergan, Rochelle, VA

PREP: 45 MIN. • **BAKE:** 35 MIN. + STANDING • **MAKES:** 12 SERVINGS

- **1 lb. bulk Italian sausage**
- **1 medium onion, chopped**
- **2 garlic cloves, minced**
- **1 can (6 oz.) tomato paste**
- **1 can (28 oz.) crushed tomatoes**
- **1 can (8 oz.) tomato sauce**
- **3 tsp. dried basil**
- **¾ tsp. pepper, divided**
- **¼ tsp. salt**
- **1 large egg, lightly beaten**
- **1 carton (15 oz.) whole-milk ricotta cheese**
- **1½ cups grated Parmesan cheese, divided**
- **12 no-cook lasagna noodles**
- **4 cups shredded part-skim mozzarella cheese**

1. Preheat oven to 400°. In a large skillet, cook and crumble sausage with onion over medium heat until no longer pink, about 5-7 minutes; drain. Add garlic and tomato paste; cook and stir 1 minute.

2. Stir in tomatoes, tomato sauce, basil, ½ tsp. pepper and salt; bring to a boil. Reduce heat; simmer, uncovered, until slightly thickened, 10-15 minutes.

3. In a bowl, mix egg, ricotta cheese, 1¼ cups Parmesan cheese and the remaining pepper. Spread 1½ cups meat sauce into a greased 13x9-in. baking dish. Layer with 4 noodles, 1½ cups ricotta cheese mixture, 1½ cups mozzarella cheese and 1½ cups sauce. Repeat layers. Top with remaining noodles, sauce and mozzarella and Parmesan cheeses.

4. Cover with greased foil; bake 30 minutes. Uncover; bake until lightly browned and heated through, 5-10 minutes. Let stand for 15 minutes before serving.

1 PIECE: 416 cal., 23g fat (11g sat. fat), 83mg chol., 978mg sod., 29g carb. (8g sugars, 3g fiber), 25g pro.

RISOTTO BALLS (ARANCINI)

My Italian grandma made these for me. I still ask for them when I visit her, and so do my children. The arancini freeze well, so I make them ahead of time.

—Gretchen Whelan, San Francisco, CA

PREP: 35 MIN. • **BAKE:** 25 MIN. • **MAKES:** ABOUT 3 DOZEN

- **1½ cups water**
- **1 cup uncooked arborio rice**
- **1 tsp. salt**
- **2 large eggs, lightly beaten**
- **⅔ cup sun-dried tomato pesto**
- **2 cups panko bread crumbs, divided**
- **Marinara sauce, warmed**

1. Preheat oven to 375°. In a large saucepan, combine water, rice and salt; bring to a boil. Reduce heat; simmer, covered, until liquid is absorbed and rice is tender, 18-20 minutes. Let stand, covered, 10 minutes. Transfer to a large bowl; cool slightly. Add eggs and pesto; stir in 1 cup bread crumbs.

2. Place remaining bread crumbs in a shallow bowl. Shape rice mixture into 1¼-in. balls. Roll in bread crumbs, patting to help coating adhere. Place on greased 15x10x1-in. baking pans. Bake until golden brown, 25-30 minutes. Serve with marinara sauce.

1 APPETIZER: 42 cal., 1g fat (0 sat. fat), 10mg chol., 125mg sod., 7g carb. (1g sugars, 0 fiber), 1g pro.

DIABETIC EXCHANGES: ½ starch.

ITALIAN PINWHEEL ROLLS

Parmesan cheese, garlic and oregano make these from-scratch rolls hard to resist. My family gets hungry when they smell them baking.

—Patricia Fitzgerald, Candor, NY

PREP: 35 MIN. + RISING • **BAKE:** 25 MIN. • **MAKES:** 1 DOZEN

- **1 pkg. (¼ oz.) active dry yeast**
- **1 cup warm water (110° to 115°)**
- **1½ tsp. sugar**
- **1½ tsp. butter, softened**
- **1 tsp. salt**
- **2¼ to 2½ cups bread flour**

FILLING

- **2 Tbsp. butter, melted**
- **¼ cup grated Parmesan cheese**
- **2 Tbsp. minced fresh parsley**
- **6 garlic cloves, minced**
- **1 tsp. dried oregano**

1. In a large bowl, dissolve yeast in warm water. Add the sugar, butter, salt and 1 cup flour; beat until smooth. Stir in enough remaining flour to form a soft dough.

2. Turn onto a floured surface; knead until smooth and elastic, 6-8 minutes. Place in a bowl coated with cooking spray, turning once to coat the top. Cover and let rise in a warm place until doubled, about 1 hour.

3. Punch dough down. Turn onto a lightly floured surface. Roll into a 12x10-in. rectangle. Brush with melted butter; sprinkle the cheese, parsley, garlic and oregano to within ½ in. of edges. Roll up jelly-roll style, starting with a long side; pinch seam to seal. Cut into 12 rolls.

4. Place rolls cut side up in a 13x9-in. baking pan coated with cooking spray. Cover and let rise until doubled, about 30 minutes.

5. Bake at 350° for 25-30 minutes or until golden brown. Remove from pan to a wire rack.

1 ROLL: 110 cal., 3g fat (2g sat. fat), 8mg chol., 253mg sod., 18g carb. (1g sugars, 1g fiber), 4g pro.

DIABETIC EXCHANGES: 1 starch, ½ fat.

ITALIAN CREAM CHEESE CAKE

Buttermilk makes every bite of this awesome Italian cream cheese cake moist and flavorful. I rely on this recipe year-round.

—Joyce Lutz, Centerview, MO

PREP: 40 MIN. • **BAKE:** 20 MIN. + COOLING • **MAKES:** 16 SERVINGS

- **½ cup butter, softened**
- **½ cup shortening**
- **2 cups sugar**
- **5 large eggs, separated, room temperature**
- **1 tsp. vanilla extract**
- **2 cups all-purpose flour**
- **1 tsp. baking soda**
- **1 cup buttermilk**
- **1½ cups sweetened shredded coconut**
- **1 cup chopped pecans**

CREAM CHEESE FROSTING

- **11 oz. cream cheese, softened**
- **¾ cup butter, softened**
- **6 cups confectioners' sugar**
- **1½ tsp. vanilla extract**
- **¾ cup chopped pecans**

1. Preheat oven to 350°. Grease and flour three 9-in. round baking pans. In a large bowl, cream butter, shortening and sugar until light and fluffy, 5-7 minutes. Beat in egg yolks and vanilla. Combine flour and baking soda; add to creamed mixture alternately with buttermilk. Beat until just combined. Stir in the coconut and pecans.

2. In another bowl, beat egg whites with clean beaters until stiff but not dry. Fold one-fourth of the egg whites into batter, then fold in remaining whites. Pour into prepared pans.

3. Bake until a toothpick inserted in center comes out clean, 20-25 minutes. Cool 10 minutes before removing from pans to wire racks to cool completely.

4. For frosting, beat cream cheese and butter until smooth. Beat in confectioners' sugar and vanilla until fluffy. Stir in pecans. Spread the frosting between layers and over top and sides of cake. Refrigerate.

1 SLICE: 736 cal., 41g fat (19g sat. fat), 117mg chol., 330mg sod., 90g carb. (75g sugars, 2g fiber), 7g pro.

Garden-Fresh Delights
• Italian Sausage-Stuffed Zucchini
• Lemon Artichoke Romaine Salad
• Swiss Cheese Bread
• Mixed Berry Tiramisu

ITALIAN SAUSAGE-STUFFED ZUCCHINI

I've always had to be creative when getting my family to eat vegetables, so I decided to make stuffed zucchini using the pizza flavors that everyone loves. It worked! We like to include sausage for a main dish but it could be a meatless side dish, too.

—Donna-Marie Ryan, Topsfield, MA

PREP: 35 MIN. • **BAKE:** 20 MIN. • **MAKES:** 6 SERVINGS

- **6 medium zucchini (about 8 oz. each)**
- **1 lb. Italian turkey sausage links, casings removed**
- **2 medium tomatoes, seeded and chopped**
- **1 cup panko bread crumbs**
- **⅓ cup grated Parmesan cheese**
- **⅓ cup minced fresh parsley**
- **2 Tbsp. minced fresh oregano or 2 tsp. dried oregano**
- **2 Tbsp. minced fresh basil or 2 tsp. dried basil**
- **¼ tsp. pepper**
- **¾ cup shredded part-skim mozzarella cheese**
- **Additional minced fresh parsley, optional**

1. Preheat oven to 350°. Cut each zucchini lengthwise in half. Scoop out pulp, leaving a ¼-in. shell; chop pulp. Place zucchini shells in a large microwave-safe dish. In batches, microwave, covered, on high 2-3 minutes or until crisp-tender.

2. In a large skillet, cook sausage and zucchini pulp over medium heat 6-8 minutes or until sausage is no longer pink, breaking sausage into crumbles; drain. Stir in tomatoes, bread crumbs, Parmesan cheese, herbs and pepper. Spoon into zucchini shells.

3. Place in 2 ungreased 13x9-in. baking dishes. Bake, covered, for 15-20 minutes or until zucchini is tender. Sprinkle with mozzarella cheese. Bake, uncovered, 5-8 minutes longer or until cheese is melted. If desired, sprinkle with additional minced parsley.

2 STUFFED ZUCCHINI HALVES: 206 cal., 9g fat (3g sat. fat), 39mg chol., 485mg sod., 16g carb. (5g sugars, 3g fiber), 17g pro.

DIABETIC EXCHANGES: 2 lean meat, 2 vegetable, ½ starch.

LEMON ARTICHOKE ROMAINE SALAD

I created this dish when I was trying to duplicate a very lemony Caesar salad. This version is not only delicious but more healthful, too.

—Kathy Armstrong, Post Falls, ID

TAKES: 15 MIN. • **MAKES:** 8 SERVINGS

- **10 cups torn romaine**
- **4 plum tomatoes, chopped**
- **1 can (14 oz.) water-packed quartered artichoke hearts, rinsed and drained**
- **1 can (2¼ oz.) sliced ripe olives, drained**
- **3 Tbsp. water**
- **3 Tbsp. lemon juice**
- **3 Tbsp. olive oil**
- **2 garlic cloves, minced**
- **1 tsp. salt**
- **1 tsp. coarsely ground pepper**
- **⅓ cup shredded Parmesan cheese**

1. Place first 4 ingredients in a large bowl. Place all remaining ingredients except cheese in a jar with a tight-fitting lid; shake well. Pour over salad; toss to coat.

2. Sprinkle with cheese. Serve immediately.

1½ CUPS: 105 cal., 7g fat (1g sat. fat), 2mg chol., 541mg sod., 8g carb. (2g sugars, 2g fiber), 4g pro.

DIABETIC EXCHANGES: 2 vegetable, 1½ fat.

SWISS CHEESE BREAD

This bread will receive rave reviews, whether you serve it as an appetizer or with a meal. For real convenience, you can make it ahead of time and freeze it.

—Karla Boice, Mahtomedi, MN

TAKES: 30 MIN. • **MAKES:** 20 SERVINGS

- **1 loaf (18-20 in.) French bread**
- **1 cup butter, softened**
- **2 cups shredded Swiss cheese**
- **¾ tsp. celery seed**
- **¾ tsp. garlic powder**
- **3 Tbsp. dried parsley flakes**

1. Cut bread in half crosswise. Make diagonal cuts, 1 in. apart, through bread but not through bottom. Combine all remaining ingredients. Spread half the butter mixture between bread slices. Spread remaining mixture over top and sides of bread.

2. Place bread on double thickness of foil; cover loosely with more foil. Bake at 425° for 20-30 minutes. For last 5 minutes, remove foil covering bread to allow it to brown.

1 SLICE: 187 cal., 13g fat (8g sat. fat), 34mg chol., 231mg sod., 12g carb. (1g sugars, 1g fiber), 6g pro.

MIXED BERRY TIRAMISU

Because I love tiramisu, I came up with this deliciously refreshing twist on the traditional coffee-flavored Italian dessert. Fresh softened berries star with crisp ladyfinger cookies and mascarpone cheese. Serve it from a glass bowl or in clear dishes to show off the luscious layers.

—Najmussahar Ahmed, Ypsilanti, MI

PREP: 35 MIN. + CHILLING • **MAKES:** 12 SERVINGS

3 cups fresh raspberries
3 cups fresh blackberries
2 cups fresh blueberries
2 cups fresh strawberries, sliced
1⅓ cups sugar, divided
4 tsp. grated orange zest
1 cup orange juice
1 cup heavy whipping cream
2 cartons (8 oz. each) mascarpone cheese
1 tsp. vanilla extract
2 pkg. (7 oz. each) crisp ladyfinger cookies
Additional fresh berries, optional

1. Place berries in a large bowl. Mix ⅓ cup sugar, orange zest and orange juice; toss gently with berries. Refrigerate, covered, 45 minutes.

2. Beat cream until soft peaks form. In another bowl, mix mascarpone cheese, vanilla and remaining sugar. Fold in whipped cream, a third at a time.

3. Drain berries over a shallow bowl, reserving juices. Dip ladyfingers in reserved juices, allowing excess to drip off; arrange in a single layer on the bottom of a 13x9-in. dish. Layer with half the berries and half the mascarpone mixture; repeat layers, starting with ladyfingers.

4. Refrigerate, covered, overnight. If desired, top with additional berries before serving.

1 PIECE: 501 cal., 26g fat (14g sat. fat), 105mg chol., 77mg sod., 63g carb. (45g sugars, 5g fiber), 8g pro.

Easy Fish Menu
• No-Fuss Fish Packets
• Green Salad with Berries
• Cheese & Garlic Biscuits
• Carrot Blueberry Cupcakes

NO-FUSS FISH PACKETS

My husband does a lot of fishing, so I'm always looking for different ways to serve his catches. A professional chef was kind enough to share this recipe with me, and I played around with some different veggie combinations until I found the one my family liked best.

—Kathy Morrow, Hubbard, OH

TAKES: 30 MIN. • **MAKES:** 4 SERVINGS

- **1 can (15 oz.) great northern beans, rinsed and drained**
- **4 plum tomatoes, chopped**
- **1 small zucchini, chopped**
- **1 medium onion, chopped**
- **1 garlic clove, minced**
- **¼ cup white wine**
- **¾ tsp. salt, divided**
- **¼ tsp. pepper, divided**
- **4 tilapia fillets (6 oz. each)**
- **1 medium lemon, cut into 8 thin slices**

1. Preheat oven to 400°. In a bowl, combine beans, tomatoes, zucchini, onion, garlic, wine, ½ tsp. salt and ⅛ tsp. pepper.

2. Rinse fish and pat dry. Place each fillet on an 18x12-in. piece of heavy-duty foil; season with remaining salt and pepper. Spoon bean mixture over fish; top with lemon slices. Fold foil around fish and crimp edges to seal. Transfer packets to a baking sheet.

3. Bake until fish just begins to flake easily with a fork and vegetables are tender, 15-20 minutes. Be careful of escaping steam when opening packets.

1 SERVING: 270 cal., 2g fat (1g sat. fat), 83mg chol., 658mg sod., 23g carb. (4g sugars, 7g fiber), 38g pro.

DIABETIC EXCHANGES: 5 lean meat, 1 starch, 1 vegetable.

GREEN SALAD WITH BERRIES

For snappy salad that draws a crowd, I do a wonderful combo of spinach, berries and onions. Raise your fork for this one.

—Aysha Schurman, Ammon, ID

TAKES: 15 MIN. • **MAKES:** 4 SERVINGS

- **1 cup torn romaine**
- **1 cup fresh baby spinach**
- **1 cup sliced fresh strawberries**
- **½ cup thinly sliced celery**
- **½ small red onion, thinly sliced**
- **½ cup coarsely chopped walnuts**
- **2 green onions, chopped**
- **¼ cup raspberry vinaigrette**
- **1 cup fresh raspberries**

In a large bowl, combine the first 7 ingredients. To serve, drizzle with vinaigrette and toss to combine. Top with raspberries.

1 SERVING: 157 cal., 10g fat (1g sat. fat), 0 chol., 50mg sod., 15g carb. (8g sugars, 5g fiber), 4g pro.

DIABETIC EXCHANGES: 2 fat, 1 vegetable, ½ fruit.

CHEESE & GARLIC BISCUITS

My biscuits won the prize for best quick bread at my county fair. One of the judges liked them so much, she asked for the recipe! These buttery, savory biscuits go with just about anything.

—Gloria Jarrett, Loveland, OH

TAKES: 20 MIN. • MAKES: 2½ DOZEN

2½ cups biscuit/baking mix
¾ cup shredded sharp cheddar cheese
1 tsp. garlic powder
1 tsp. ranch salad dressing mix
1 cup buttermilk

TOPPING
½ cup butter, melted
1 Tbsp. minced chives
½ tsp. garlic powder
½ tsp. ranch salad dressing mix
¼ tsp. pepper

1. In a large bowl, combine the baking mix, cheese, garlic powder and salad dressing mix. Stir in buttermilk just until moistened. Drop by tablespoonfuls onto greased baking sheets.

2. Bake at 450° until golden brown, 6-8 minutes. Meanwhile, combine topping ingredients. Brush over biscuits. Serve warm.

1 BISCUIT: 81 cal., 5g fat (3g sat. fat), 11mg chol., 176mg sod., 7g carb. (1g sugars, 0 fiber), 2g pro.

CARROT BLUEBERRY CUPCAKES

Carrots, blueberries, pineapple and zucchini make an interesting and delicious combination in these unique little treats.

—Patricia Kile, Elizabethtown, PA

PREP: 35 MIN. • **BAKE:** 20 MIN. + COOLING • **MAKES:** 16 CUPCAKES

- 1 cup sugar
- ½ cup canola oil
- 2 large eggs, room temperature
- 1 tsp. vanilla extract
- 1½ cups all-purpose flour
- 1 tsp. baking powder
- 1 tsp. ground cinnamon
- ½ tsp. baking soda
- ½ tsp. salt
- 1 cup finely shredded carrots
- ¾ cup grated zucchini
- ½ cup unsweetened crushed pineapple, drained
- 1 cup fresh or frozen unsweetened blueberries

FROSTING

- 3 oz. cream cheese, softened
- ¼ cup butter, softened
- 2½ cups confectioners' sugar
- 1 tsp. vanilla extract
- ½ cup chopped pecans, optional
- Fresh blueberries, optional

1. In a small bowl, beat the sugar, oil, eggs and vanilla. In another large bowl, combine the flour, baking powder, cinnamon, baking soda and salt; gradually beat into sugar mixture until blended. Stir in the carrots, zucchini and pineapple. Fold in blueberries.

2. Fill paper-lined muffin cups two-thirds full. Bake at 375° for 18-22 minutes or until a toothpick inserted in the center comes out clean. Cool for 10 minutes before removing from pans to wire racks to cool completely.

3. For frosting, in a large bowl, beat cream cheese and butter until fluffy. Add confectioners' sugar and vanilla; beat until smooth. Frost cupcakes. If desired, top with nuts and fresh blueberries. Refrigerate leftovers.

1 CUPCAKE: 294 cal., 13g fat (4g sat. fat), 40mg chol., 189mg sod., 44g carb. (33g sugars, 1g fiber), 3g pro.

CHAPTER 2

ONE-DISH SUNDAY DINNERS

When it comes to comfort and convenience, few recipes can top a meal-in-one specialty. Get cozy any time of year with these hearty dishes that are guaranteed to satisfy.

SLICED HAM WITH ROASTED VEGETABLES

To prepare this colorful, zesty oven meal, I shop in my backyard for the fresh garden vegetables and oranges (we have our own tree!) that spark the ham's hearty flavor. It's my family's favorite dinner.

—Margaret Pache, Mesa, AZ

PREP: 10 MIN. • **BAKE:** 35 MIN. • **MAKES:** 6 SERVINGS

Cooking spray
6 medium potatoes, peeled and cubed
5 medium carrots, sliced
1 medium turnip, peeled and cubed
1 large onion, cut into thin wedges
6 slices (4 to 6 oz. each) fully cooked ham, halved
¼ cup thawed orange juice concentrate
2 Tbsp. brown sugar
1 tsp. prepared horseradish
1 tsp. grated orange zest
Coarsely ground pepper

1. Grease two 15x10x1-in. baking pans with cooking spray. Add the potatoes, carrots, turnip and onion; generously coat with cooking spray. Bake, uncovered, at 425° until vegetables are tender, 25-30 minutes.

2. Arrange ham slices over the vegetables. In a bowl, combine concentrate, brown sugar, horseradish and orange zest. Spoon over ham and vegetables. Bake until the ham is heated through, about 10 minutes longer. Sprinkle with pepper.

1 SERVING: 375 cal., 5g fat (1g sat. fat), 71mg chol., 1179mg sod., 55g carb. (15g sugars, 7g fiber), 31g pro.

Southern Living

CHICKEN MARSALA LASAGNA

I love chicken Marsala, but most recipes do not serve a crowd. So I invented this version, which makes enough for 12 people. It's perfect for a Sunday dinner.

—Debbie Shannon, Ringgold, GA

PREP: 50 MIN. • **BAKE:** 50 MIN. + STANDING • **MAKES:** 12 SERVINGS

- **12 lasagna noodles**
- **4 tsp. Italian seasoning, divided**
- **1 tsp. salt**
- **¾ lb. boneless skinless chicken breasts, cubed**
- **1 Tbsp. olive oil**
- **¼ cup finely chopped onion**
- **½ cup butter, cubed**
- **½ lb. sliced baby portobello mushrooms**
- **12 garlic cloves, minced**
- **1½ cups beef broth**
- **¾ cup Marsala wine, divided**
- **¼ tsp. coarsely ground pepper**
- **3 Tbsp. cornstarch**
- **½ cup finely chopped fully cooked ham**
- **1 carton (15 oz.) ricotta cheese**
- **1 pkg. (10 oz.) frozen chopped spinach, thawed and squeezed dry**
- **2 cups shredded Italian cheese blend**
- **1 cup grated Parmesan cheese, divided**
- **2 large eggs, lightly beaten**

1. Cook noodles according to package directions; drain. Meanwhile, mix 2 tsp. Italian seasoning and salt; sprinkle over chicken breasts. In a large skillet, heat olive oil over medium-high heat. Add chicken; saute until no longer pink. Remove and keep warm.

2. In same skillet, cook onion in butter over medium heat for 2 minutes. Stir in mushrooms; cook until tender, 4-5 minutes longer. Add garlic; cook and stir 2 minutes.

3. Stir in broth, ½ cup wine and pepper; bring to a boil. Mix cornstarch and remaining wine until smooth; stir into pan. Bring to a boil; cook and stir until thickened, about 2 minutes. Stir in ham and chicken.

4. Preheat oven to 350°. Combine ricotta cheese, spinach, Italian cheese blend, ¾ cup Parmesan cheese, eggs and remaining Italian seasoning. Spread 1 cup chicken mixture into a greased 13x9-in. baking dish. Layer with 3 noodles, about ¾ cup chicken mixture and about 1 cup ricotta mixture. Repeat layers 3 times.

5. Bake, covered, 40 minutes. Sprinkle with the remaining Parmesan cheese. Bake, uncovered, until casserole is bubbly and cheese is melted, 10-15 minutes. Let stand 10 minutes before cutting.

FREEZE OPTION: Cool unbaked lasagna; cover and freeze. To use, partially thaw in refrigerator overnight. Remove from refrigerator 30 minutes before baking. Preheat oven to 350°. Cover lasagna with foil; bake as directed until heated through and a thermometer inserted into the center reads 165°, increasing time to 45-50 minutes. Sprinkle with remaining Parmesan cheese. Bake, uncovered, until casserole is bubbly and cheese is melted, 10-15 minutes. Let stand 10 minutes before cutting.

1 PIECE: 388 cal., 20 g fat (12 g sat. fat), 107 mg chol., 749 mg sod., 27 g carb., 2 g fiber, 24 g pro.

BEEF & BACON GNOCCHI SKILLET

This gnocchi dish tastes like a bacon cheeseburger. Go ahead and top it as you would a burger—with ketchup, mustard and pickles.

—Ashley Lecker, Green Bay, WI

TAKES: 30 MIN. • **MAKES:** 6 SERVINGS

- **1 pkg. (16 oz.) potato gnocchi**
- **1¼ lbs. lean ground beef (90% lean)**
- **1 medium onion, chopped**
- **8 cooked bacon strips, crumbled and divided**
- **1 cup water**
- **½ cup heavy whipping cream**
- **1 Tbsp. ketchup**
- **¼ tsp. salt**
- **¼ tsp. pepper**
- **1½ cups shredded cheddar cheese**
- **½ cup chopped tomatoes**
- **2 green onions, sliced**

1. Preheat broiler. Cook gnocchi according to package directions; drain.

2. Meanwhile, in a large cast-iron or other ovenproof skillet, cook beef and onion over medium heat until beef is no longer pink, 4-6 minutes, breaking meat into crumbles. Drain.

3. Stir in half the bacon; add gnocchi, water, cream and ketchup. Bring to a boil. Cook, stirring, over medium heat until the sauce has thickened, 3-4 minutes. Add the salt and pepper. Sprinkle with cheese.

4. Broil 3-4 in. from heat until cheese has melted, 1-2 minutes. Top with tomatoes, green onions and remaining bacon.

1 CUP: 573 cal., 31g fat (16g sat. fat), 136mg chol., 961mg sod., 35g carb. (7g sugars, 2g fiber), 36g pro.

SERVE WITH:
Red & Green Salad with Toasted Almonds, Page 216

RAVIOLI WITH CREAMY SQUASH SAUCE

Store-bought ravioli speeds assembly of this cozy, restaurant-quality dish. It tastes so good, your family won't notice it's meatless.

—Taste of Home *Test Kitchen*

TAKES: 20 MIN. • MAKES: 4 SERVINGS

- **1 pkg. (9 oz.) refrigerated cheese ravioli**
- **3 garlic cloves, minced**
- **2 Tbsp. butter**
- **1 pkg. (10 oz.) frozen cooked winter squash, thawed**
- **1 pkg. (6 oz.) fresh baby spinach**
- **1 cup heavy whipping cream**
- **⅓ cup vegetable broth**
- **¼ tsp. salt**
- **1 cup chopped walnuts, toasted**

1. Cook ravioli according to package directions. Meanwhile, in a Dutch oven, saute garlic in butter for 1 minute. Add the squash and spinach; cook 2-3 minutes longer or until the spinach is wilted. Stir in cream, broth and salt. Bring to a gentle boil; cook for 6-8 minutes or until slightly thickened.

2. Drain ravioli; add to squash mixture. Toss to coat. Sprinkle with walnuts.

1¼ CUPS: 671 cal., 51g fat (22g sat. fat), 122mg chol., 578mg sod., 42g carb. (2g sugars, 7g fiber), 18g pro.

GLAZED SMOKED CHOPS WITH PEARS

My husband would eat pork chops every day if he could. Luckily, they're good all sorts of ways, including with pears.

—Lynn Moretti, Oconomowoc, WI

TAKES: 30 MIN. • **MAKES:** 4 SERVINGS

- **4 smoked boneless pork chops**
- **1 Tbsp. olive oil**
- **1 large sweet onion, cut into thin wedges**
- **½ cup dry red wine or reduced-sodium chicken broth**
- **2 Tbsp. balsamic vinegar**
- **2 Tbsp. honey**
- **2 large ripe pears, cut into 1-in. wedges**

1. Preheat oven to 350°. In an ovenproof skillet over medium-high heat, brown pork chops on both sides; remove from pan.

2. In same pan, heat oil over medium heat; saute onion until tender, 3-5 minutes. Add wine, vinegar and honey; bring to a boil, stirring to loosen browned bits from pan. Reduce heat; simmer, uncovered, until slightly thickened, about 5 minutes, stirring occasionally.

3. Return chops to pan; top with pears. Transfer to oven; bake until pears are tender, 10-15 minutes.

1 SERVING: 313 cal., 4g fat (6g sat. fat), 41mg chol., 1056mg sod., 34g carb. (26g sugars, 4g fiber), 22g pro.

INDIVIDUAL SHEPHERD'S PIES

These comforting little pies make a fun surprise for the family. Extras are easy to freeze and eat later on busy weeknights.

—Ellen Osborne, Clarksville, TN

PREP: 30 MIN. • **BAKE:** 20 MIN. • **MAKES:** 10 MINI PIES

- **1 lb. ground beef**
- **3 Tbsp. chopped onion**
- **½ tsp. minced garlic**
- **⅓ cup chili sauce or ketchup**
- **1 Tbsp. cider vinegar**
- **2 cups hot mashed potatoes (with added milk and butter)**
- **3 oz. cream cheese, softened**
- **1 tube (12 oz.) refrigerated buttermilk biscuits**
- **½ cup crushed potato chips**
- **Paprika, optional**

1. Preheat oven to 375°. In a large skillet, cook beef and onion over medium heat until beef is no longer pink, 5-7 minutes, breaking up beef into crumbles. Add garlic; cook 1 minute or until tender. Drain. Stir in chili sauce and vinegar.

2. In a small bowl, mix mashed potatoes and cream cheese until blended. Press 1 biscuit onto bottom and up sides of each of 10 greased muffin cups. Fill with beef mixture. Spread the potato mixture over the tops. Sprinkle with crushed potato chips, pressing down lightly.

3. Bake until golden brown, 20-25 minutes. If desired, sprinkle with paprika.

FREEZE OPTION: Freeze cooled shepherd's pies in a single layer in freezer containers. To use, partially thaw in refrigerator overnight. Bake on a baking sheet in a preheated 375° oven until heated through, 15-18 minutes.

2 MINI PIES: 567 cal., 30g fat (12g sat. fat), 84mg chol., 1378mg sod., 51g carb. (9g sugars, 2g fiber), 23g pro.

SAUSAGE & SQUASH PENNE

I love using frozen cooked winter squash because the hard work—peeling, chopping and cooking—is all done for me.

—Jennifer Roberts, South Burlington, VT

TAKES: 30 MIN. • **MAKES:** 4 SERVINGS

- **2 cups uncooked penne pasta**
- **1 pkg. (12 oz.) frozen cooked winter squash**
- **2 Tbsp. olive oil**
- **3 cooked Italian sausage links (4 oz. each), sliced**
- **1 medium onion, chopped**
- **¼ cup grated Parmesan cheese**
- **¼ tsp. salt**
- **¼ tsp. dried parsley flakes**
- **¼ tsp. pepper**
- **Optional: Additional grated Parmesan cheese and minced fresh parsley**

1. Cook pasta and squash according to package directions. Meanwhile, in a large skillet, heat oil over medium heat. Add sausage and onion; cook and stir until sausage is browned and onion is tender; keep warm.

2. In a small bowl, mix the cooked squash, cheese, salt, parsley and pepper until blended. Drain pasta; transfer to a serving plate. Spoon squash mixture over pasta; top with sausage mixture. If desired, sprinkle with additional cheese and parsley.

¾ CUP PASTA WITH ½ CUP SAUSAGE AND ¼ CUP SQUASH: 468 cal., 26g fat (8g sat. fat), 40mg chol., 705mg sod., 41g carb. (4g sugars, 4g fiber), 19g pro.

PUFF PASTRY CHICKEN POTPIE

When my wife is craving comfort food, I whip up my chicken potpie. It's easy to make, sticks to your ribs and delivers soul-satisfying flavor.

—Nick Iverson, Denver, CO

PREP: 45 MIN. • **BAKE:** 45 MIN. + STANDING • **MAKES:** 8 SERVINGS

- **1 pkg. (17.3 oz.) frozen puff pastry, thawed**
- **2 lbs. boneless skinless chicken breasts, cut into 1-in. pieces**
- **1 tsp. salt, divided**
- **1 tsp. pepper, divided**
- **4 Tbsp. butter, divided**
- **1 large onion, chopped**
- **2 garlic cloves, minced**
- **1 tsp. minced fresh thyme or ¼ tsp. dried thyme**
- **1 tsp. minced fresh sage or ¼ tsp. rubbed sage**
- **½ cup all-purpose flour**
- **1½ cups chicken broth**
- **1 cup plus 1 Tbsp. half-and-half cream, divided**
- **2 cups frozen mixed vegetables (about 10 oz.)**
- **1 Tbsp. lemon juice**
- **1 large egg yolk**

1. Preheat oven to 400°. On a lightly floured surface, roll each pastry sheet into a 12x10-in. rectangle. Cut 1 sheet crosswise into six 2-in. strips; cut remaining sheet lengthwise into five 2-in. strips. On a baking sheet, closely weave strips to make a 12x10-in. lattice. Freeze while making filling.

2. Toss chicken with ½ tsp. each salt and pepper. In a large skillet, heat 1 Tbsp. butter over medium-high heat; saute chicken until browned, 5-7 minutes. Remove from pan.

3. In same skillet, heat remaining butter over medium-high heat; saute onion until tender, 5-7 minutes. Stir in garlic and herbs; cook 1 minute. Stir in flour until blended; cook and stir 1 minute. Gradually stir in broth and 1 cup cream. Bring to a boil, stirring constantly; cook and stir until thickened, about 2 minutes.

4. Stir in vegetables, lemon juice, chicken and the remaining salt and pepper; return to a boil. Transfer to a greased 2½-qt. oblong baking dish. Top with lattice, trimming to fit.

5. Whisk together egg yolk and remaining cream; brush over the pastry. Bake, uncovered, until bubbly and golden brown, 45-55 minutes. Cover loosely with foil if pastry starts getting too dark. Let stand 15 minutes before serving.

1 SERVING: 523 cal., 25g fat (10g sat. fat), 118mg chol., 768mg sod., 42g carb. (4g sugars, 6g fiber), 30g pro.

KITCHEN TIP: For a crisper crust, trim lattice to fit your baking dish, then place the crust on a parchment-lined baking sheet. Bake at 400° for 20-25 minutes. Gently place crust on top of the hot filling before serving.

SLOW-COOKED PORK STEW

Try this comforting stew that's easy to put together, but tastes like you've been working hard in the kitchen all day. It's even better served over polenta, egg noodles or mashed potatoes.

—Nancy Elliott, Houston, TX

PREP: 15 MIN. • **COOK:** 5 HOURS • **MAKES:** 8 SERVINGS

- **2 pork tenderloins (1 lb. each), cut into 2-in. pieces**
- **1 tsp. salt**
- **½ tsp. pepper**
- **2 large carrots, cut into ½-in. slices**
- **2 celery ribs, coarsely chopped**
- **1 medium onion, coarsely chopped**
- **3 cups beef broth**
- **2 Tbsp. tomato paste**
- **⅓ cup pitted dried plums (prunes), chopped**
- **4 garlic cloves, minced**
- **2 bay leaves**
- **1 fresh rosemary sprig**
- **1 fresh thyme sprig**
- **⅓ cup Greek olives, optional**
- **Chopped fresh parsley, optional**
- **Hot cooked mashed potatoes, optional**

SERVE WITH:
Herb Quick Bread, Page 224

1. Sprinkle pork with salt and pepper; transfer to a 4-qt. slow cooker. Add carrots, celery and onion. In a small bowl, whisk broth and tomato paste; pour over vegetables. Add the plums, garlic, bay leaves, rosemary, thyme and, if desired, olives. Cook, covered, on low 5-6 hours or until the meat and the vegetables are tender.

2. Discard bay leaves, rosemary and thyme. If desired, sprinkle stew with parsley and serve with potatoes.

1 CUP: 177 cal., 4g fat (1g sat. fat), 64mg chol., 698mg sod., 9g carb. (4g sugars, 1g fiber), 24g pro.

DIABETIC EXCHANGES: 3 lean meat, ½ starch.

HOT SURFACE
Hamilton Beach
OFF
LOW
HIGH

TILAPIA WITH CORN SALSA

My family loves fish, and this super fast dish is very popular at my house. Though it tastes as if it takes a long time, it cooks in minutes under the broiler. We like it garnished with lemon wedges and served with couscous on the side.

—Brenda Coffey, Singer Island, FL

TAKES: 10 MIN. • **MAKES:** 4 SERVINGS

- **4 tilapia fillets (6 oz. each)**
- **1 Tbsp. olive oil**
- **¼ tsp. salt**
- **¼ tsp. pepper**
- **1 can (15 oz.) black beans, rinsed and drained**
- **1 can (11 oz.) whole kernel corn, drained**
- **½ cup Italian salad dressing**
- **2 Tbsp. chopped green onion**
- **2 Tbsp. chopped sweet red pepper**

1. Drizzle both sides of the fillets with oil; sprinkle with salt and pepper.

2. Broil 4-6 in. from the heat until fish flakes easily with a fork, 5-7 minutes. Meanwhile, in a small bowl, combine remaining ingredients. Serve with fish.

1 FILLET WITH ¾ CUP SALSA: 354 cal., 10g fat (2g sat. fat), 83mg chol., 934mg sod., 25g carb. (7g sugars, 6g fiber), 38g pro.

NEW ENGLAND BEAN & BOG CASSOULET

When I moved to New England, I embraced the local cuisine. My cassoulet with baked beans pays tribute to a French classic and to New England.

—Devon Delaney, Westport, CT

PREP: 15 MIN. • **COOK:** 35 MIN. • **MAKES:** 8 SERVINGS (3½ QT.)

- **5 Tbsp. olive oil, divided**
- **8 boneless skinless chicken thighs (about 2 lbs.)**
- **1 pkg. (12 oz.) fully cooked Italian chicken sausage links, cut into ½-in. slices**
- **4 shallots, finely chopped**
- **2 tsp. minced fresh rosemary or ½ tsp. dried rosemary, crushed**
- **2 tsp. minced fresh thyme or ½ tsp. dried thyme**
- **1 can (28 oz.) fire-roasted diced tomatoes, undrained**
- **1 can (16 oz.) baked beans**
- **1 cup chicken broth**
- **½ cup fresh or frozen cranberries**
- **3 day-old croissants, cubed (about 6 cups)**
- **½ tsp. lemon-pepper seasoning**
- **2 Tbsp. minced fresh parsley**

1. Preheat oven to 400°. In a Dutch oven, heat 2 Tbsp. oil over medium heat. In batches, brown chicken thighs on both sides; remove from pan, reserving drippings. Add sausage; cook and stir until lightly browned. Remove from pan.

2. In same pan, heat 1 Tbsp. oil over medium heat. Add shallots, rosemary and thyme; cook and stir until shallots are tender, 1-2 minutes. Stir in the tomatoes, beans, broth and cranberries. Return chicken and sausage to pan; bring to a boil. Bake, covered, until chicken is tender, 20-25 minutes.

3. Toss croissant pieces with remaining oil; sprinkle with lemon pepper. Arrange over chicken mixture. Bake, uncovered, until croissants are golden brown, 12-15 minutes. Sprinkle with minced parsley.

1¾ CUPS: 500 cal., 26g fat (7g sat. fat), 127mg chol., 1050mg sod., 32g carb. (6g sugars, 5g fiber), 35g pro.

TAMALE PIE

The amount of spice in this recipe is just right for my family—we prefer things on the mild side. Make it once with these measurements, then spice it up a little more if you like!

—Ruth Aden, Polson, MT

PREP: 35 MIN. • **BAKE:** 30 MIN. • **MAKES:** 8 SERVINGS

- **1½ lbs. ground beef**
- **2 cans (14½ oz. each) stewed tomatoes**
- **1 medium onion, chopped**
- **½ tsp. garlic powder**
- **½ tsp. chili powder**
- **¼ tsp. salt**
- **¼ tsp. pepper**
- **10 flour tortillas (6 in.)**
- **3 cups (12 oz. each) shredded cheddar-Monterey Jack cheese or Colby-Jack cheese**
- **1 can (2¼ oz.) sliced ripe olives, drained**

SERVE WITH:
Agua de Jamaica, Page 58

1. In a skillet, brown ground beef; drain. Add tomatoes, onion and spices. Simmer, uncovered, for 20 minutes.

2. Arrange 5 tortillas in the bottom of a 13x9-in. baking dish, tearing tortillas as needed. Cover with half of the meat mixture, then half of the cheese. Repeat layers, using remaining tortillas, meat mixture and cheese. Sprinkle with olives.

3. Bake at 350° for 30 minutes or until heated through. Let stand a few minutes before serving.

1 PIECE: 428 cal., 24g fat (13g sat. fat), 79mg chol., 829mg sod., 24g carb. (4g sugars, 1g fiber), 29g pro.

BALSAMIC BRAISED POT ROAST

Pot roast can be an easy, elegant way to serve a relatively inexpensive cut of meat, so I have spent years perfecting this recipe. Believe it or not, there is an art to perfect pot roast, and every time I make this, adults and kids alike gobble it up quickly.

—Kelly Anderson, Glendale, CA

PREP: 40 MIN. • **BAKE:** 2½ HOURS • **MAKES:** 8 SERVINGS

- **1 boneless beef chuck roast (3 to 4 lbs.)**
- **1 tsp. salt**
- **½ tsp. pepper**
- **2 Tbsp. olive oil**
- **3 celery ribs with leaves, cut into 2-in. pieces**
- **2 medium carrots, cut into 1-in. pieces**
- **1 medium onion, cut into wedges**
- **3 medium turnips, peeled and quartered**
- **1 large sweet potato, peeled and cubed**
- **3 garlic cloves, minced**
- **1 cup dry red wine or beef broth**
- **1 can (14½ oz.) beef broth**
- **½ cup balsamic vinegar**
- **1 small bunch fresh thyme sprigs**
- **4 fresh sage leaves**
- **2 bay leaves**
- **¼ cup cornstarch**
- **¼ cup cold water**

1. Preheat oven to 325°. Sprinkle roast with salt and pepper. In a Dutch oven, heat oil over medium heat. Brown roast on all sides. Remove from pot.

2. Add celery, carrots and onion to the pot; cook and stir 3-4 minutes or until fragrant. Add turnips, sweet potato and garlic; cook 1 minute longer.

3. Add wine, stirring to loosen browned bits from pot. Stir in broth, vinegar and herbs. Return roast to pot; bring to a boil. Bake, covered, 2½ to 3 hours or until meat is tender.

4. Remove beef and vegetables; keep warm. Discard herbs from cooking juices; skim fat. In a small bowl, mix cornstarch and water until smooth; stir into cooking juices. Bring to a boil; cook and stir 2 minutes or until thickened. Serve with the pot roast and vegetables.

4 OZ. COOKED BEEF WITH 1 CUP VEGETABLES AND ½ CUP GRAVY: 405 cal., 20g fat (7g sat. fat), 111mg chol., 657mg sod., 19g carb. (9g sugars, 3g fiber), 35g pro.

THIS MIDWESTERN TREND IS AMAZING NEWS FOR PIZZA LOVERS

FOR FRESH, HYPERLOCAL PIES, HEAD TO A PIZZA FARM.

It's Friday night and you're in the mood for pizza. Sure, you could call in a delivery order, pop a frozen pizza in the oven or head over to a neighborhood joint for some pie. But if you're in the Midwest, why not try out a pizza farm?

WHAT IS A PIZZA FARM?

If you haven't heard of this fun new trend, it's pretty simple. Select farms across Wisconsin, Minnesota, Iowa and other Midwest states have begun inviting folks to their homesteads for a night of good food in the great outdoors...and pizza lovers are clamoring for the experience.

To learn more about the pizza-farm craze, the team at *Taste of Home* traveled to Stoney Acres Farm just outside of Wausau, Wisconsin. We chatted with owner Tony Schultz about life on a farm, the local food movement and the secret to amazing pizza.

GETTING STARTED

Founded in 1948 by Schultz's grandfather, Stoney Acres Farm has been in the family for more than 70 years. It started out as a dairy farm, but in 2006, Schultz bought the farm from his parents and started to grow organic produce.

He was inspired by the Community-Supported Agriculture (CSA) movement he saw in nearby Madison, Wisconsin, and felt that Wausau could support a similar program.

Left: No one imagined that Stoney Acres Farm would become the best pizzeria in town.
Above: Beth Howard prepares another of the farm's popular pies.

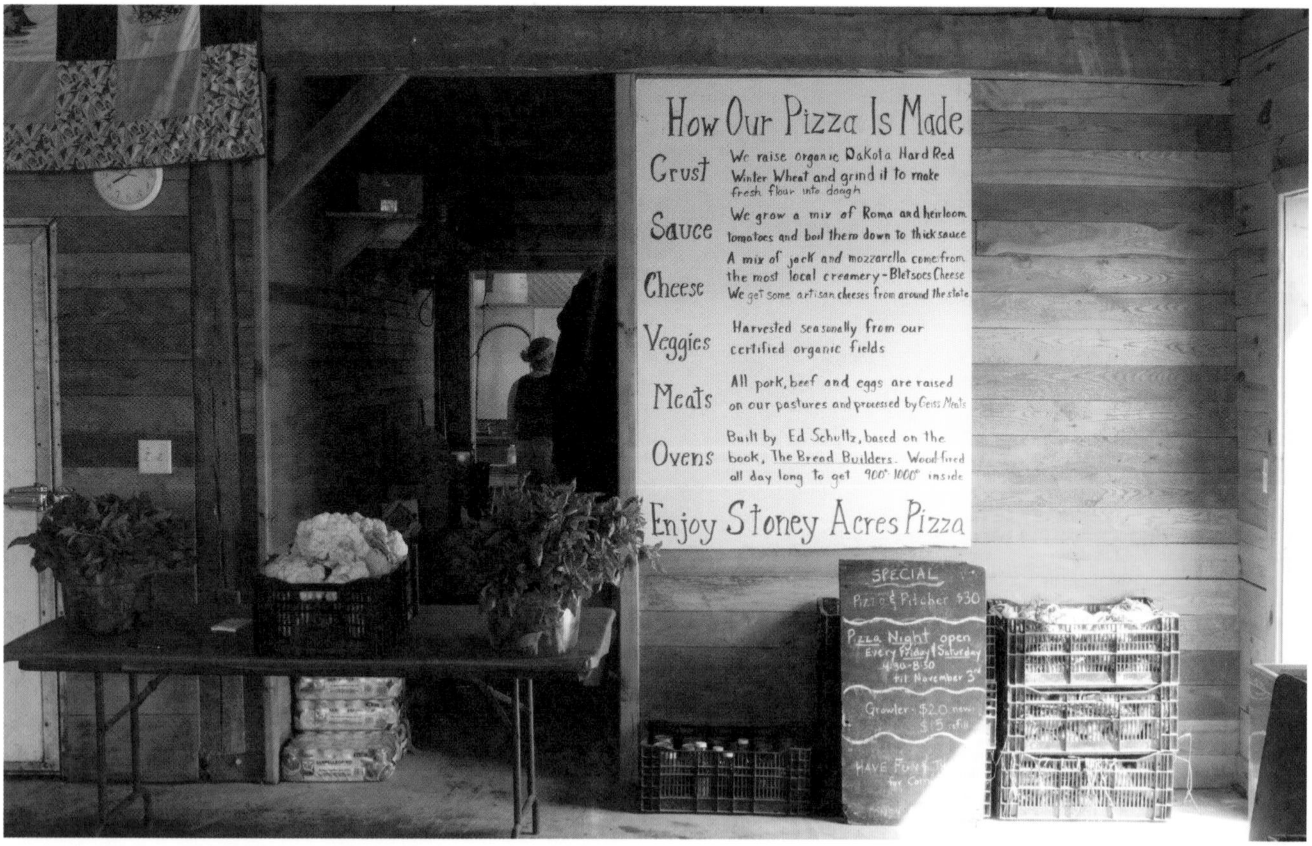
How Our Pizza Is Made
Crust
We raise organic Dakota Hard Red Winter Wheat and grind it to make fresh flour into dough
Sauce
We grow a mix of Roma and heirloom tomatoes and boil them down to thick sauce
Cheese
A mix of jack and mozzarella come from the most local creamery - Bletsoes Cheese
We get some artisan cheeses from around the state
Veggies
Harvested seasonally from our certified organic fields
Meats
All pork, beef and eggs are raised on our pastures and processed by Geiss Meats
Ovens
Built by Ed Schultz, based on the book, The Bread Builders. Wood fired all day long to get 900°-1000° inside
Enjoy Stoney Acres Pizza
SPECIAL
Pizza & Pitcher $30
Pizza Night open
Every Friday & Saturday
4:30-8:30
til November 3rd
Growler - $20 new
$5 refill

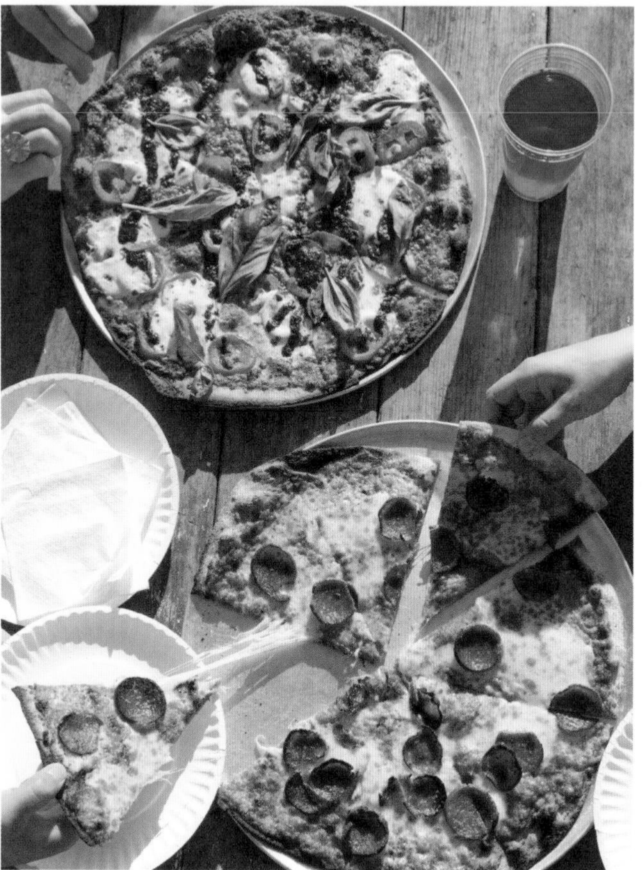

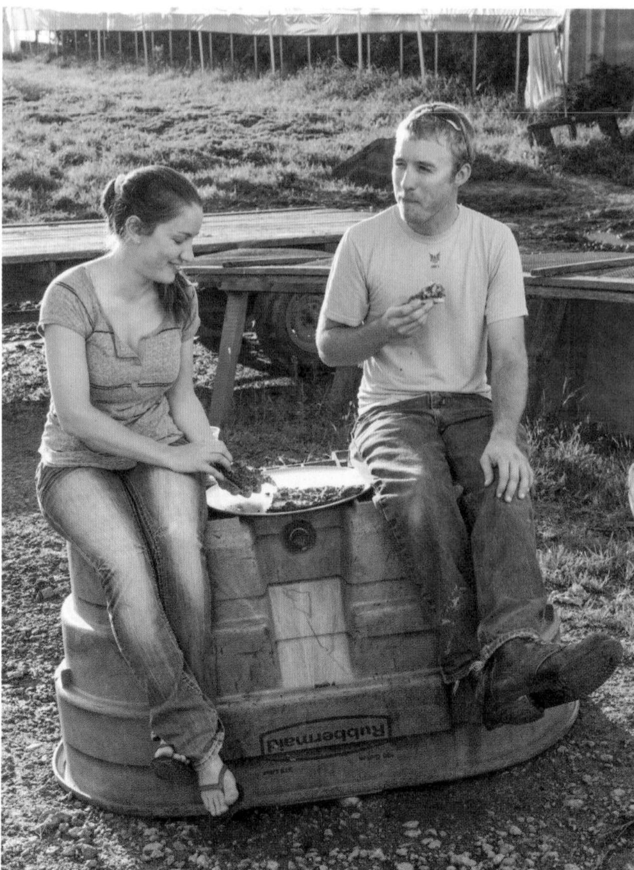

Stoney Acres began to host farm events, and in 2010 Schultz built a hearth. By 2012, pizza nights were open to the public.

GROWING THE INGREDIENTS

The main appeal of a pizza farm is that all the ingredients are local. At Stoney Acres, Schultz grows wheat, tomatoes and almost all the toppings. "The only thing we're not doing is cheese," Schultz says. "But I get that from my neighbor. It's from the nearest creamery, so it's hyperlocal."

When making a pizza, the first step is the dough. Schultz raises a Dakota hard red wheat, grinds it into flour (typically the morning of a pizza night) and then forms the dough.

Next, he makes the sauce. "We gather a lot of San Marzano tomatoes out of the field, particularly in early September when they're at the peak of their season," Schultz says. "That's the main part of my sauce, but I also harvest heirlooms. So any leftover heirlooms...they get chopped up and blended into the sauce as well."

Schultz's cheese comes from a handful of local Wisconsin farms. His main blend of Monterey Jack and mozzarella cheese comes from a creamery in Little Chicago, Wisconsin, which is a simple 15-minute drive from the farm. Depending on availability, Schultz will get Parmesan, Glacier Blue and other artisan cheeses from creameries around the state.

As far as toppings go, Schultz grows mushrooms, peppers, eggplants, greens—all sorts of veggies. He also raises pigs that get turned into sausage, bacon and pepperoni.

No matter the pie, every single ingredient that goes into or onto the pizza is farm-raised, and Schultz believes that's what makes all the difference. "That's a big part of what makes pizza on the farm not just this sort of novel idea, but what makes it really good pizza," Schultz says. "The ingredients are super fresh. We harvest in the morning, we prep it in the afternoon and we put it on a pizza at 4 o'clock."

MAKING THE PIE

At Stoney Acres, the menu is always a little different. Schultz has four types of pizza on the menu—cheese, pepperoni, sausage and veggie—plus a few rotating specials. But the exact ingredients on the pie depend on the season. "At the beginning of the year it's more lighter greens," Schultz says. "At other times, we rely on a lot of beautiful peppers, tomatoes, caramelized onions, roasted eggplant, etc."

The rotating specials depend on availability and Schultz's creativity. He plans the pies around "whatever's coming out of the field" and whatever he's inspired by. His favorite ingredient to use is one that you've likely never even heard of: Marathon Red Clover. The clover grows naturally in Marathon County, where Stoney Acres is located, and Schultz thinks it's the perfect garnish.

In addition to the specialized ingredients, Schultz's rotating specials have fun names. The Betty Draper—inspired by the *Mad Men* character—is a pie made with bacon, roasted eggplant and caramelized onions, then garnished with microgreens and local Parmesan.

The It's All Clover Now Baby Blue pie features sausage, kale, pesto, blue cheese and a garnish of Marathon Red Clover. The name is a riff on a classic Bob Dylan song—and Schultz jokes that any patron who can make the connection gets $1 off his pie.

Take a cue from the team at Stoney Acres Farm and surprise your family with a from-scratch pizza tonight. Simply turn the page for the recipe for a fresh finger-licking pie, and get ready to call your crew to the dinner table.

SMOKY GRILLED PIZZA WITH GREENS & TOMATOES

This smoky grilled pizza scores big with me for two reasons: It encourages my husband and son to eat greens, and it showcases fresh produce.

—Sarah Gray, Erie, CO

PREP: 15 MIN. + RISING • **GRILL:** 10 MIN. • **MAKES:** 2 PIZZAS (4 PIECES EACH)

- **3 cups all-purpose flour**
- **2 tsp. kosher salt**
- **1 tsp. active dry yeast**
- **3 Tbsp. olive oil, divided**
- **1¼ to 1½ cups warm water (120° to 130°)**

TOPPING

- **2 Tbsp. olive oil**
- **10 cups beet greens, coarsely chopped**
- **4 garlic cloves, minced**
- **2 Tbsp. balsamic vinegar**
- **¾ cup prepared pesto**
- **¾ cup shredded Italian cheese blend**
- **½ cup crumbled feta cheese**
- **2 medium heirloom tomatoes, thinly sliced**
- **¼ cup fresh basil leaves, chopped**

1. Place flour, salt and yeast in a food processor; pulse until blended. While processing, add 2 Tbsp. oil and enough water in a steady stream for dough to form a ball. Turn dough onto a floured surface; knead until smooth and elastic, 6-8 minutes.

2. Place in a greased bowl, turning once to grease the top. Cover dough and let rise in a warm place until almost doubled, about 1½ hours.

3. Punch down dough. On a lightly floured surface, divide dough into 2 portions. Press or roll each portion into a 10-in. circle; place each on a piece of greased foil (about 12 in. square). Brush tops with remaining oil; cover and let rest 10 minutes.

4. For topping, in a 6-qt. stockpot, heat oil over medium-high heat. Add beet greens; cook and stir until tender, 3-5 minutes. Add the garlic; cook 30 seconds longer. Remove from heat; stir in vinegar.

5. Carefully invert pizza crusts onto oiled grill rack; remove foil. Grill, covered, over medium heat until bottoms are lightly browned, 3-5 minutes. Turn; grill until second side begins to brown, 1-2 minutes.

6. Remove from grill. Spread with pesto; top with beet greens, cheeses and tomatoes. Return pizzas to grill. Cook, covered, over medium heat until cheese is melted, 2-4 minutes. Sprinkle with basil.

1 PIECE: 407 cal., 20g fat (5g sat. fat), 11mg chol., 1007mg sod., 44g carb. (3g sugars, 4g fiber), 11g pro.

CHAPTER 3

FAVORITE FARMHOUSE ENTREES

Few things celebrate the comfort of togetherness like a Sunday dinner with those you love. From golden roast chicken and succulent beef tenderloin to hearty meat pies and finger-licking ribs slathered in sauce, the down-home specialties found here promise to make memories around your table.

CHICKEN & GOAT CHEESE SKILLET

My husband was completely bowled over by this on-a-whim skillet meal. I can't wait to make it again very soon!

—Ericka Barber, Eureka, CA

TAKES: 20 MIN. • **MAKES:** 2 SERVINGS

- **½ lb. boneless skinless chicken breasts, cut into 1-in. pieces**
- **¼ tsp. salt**
- **⅛ tsp. pepper**
- **2 tsp. olive oil**
- **1 cup cut fresh asparagus (1-in. pieces)**
- **1 garlic clove, minced**
- **3 plum tomatoes, chopped**
- **3 Tbsp. 2% milk**
- **2 Tbsp. herbed fresh goat cheese, crumbled**
- **Hot cooked rice or pasta**
- **Additional goat cheese, optional**

1. Toss chicken with salt and pepper. In a large skillet, heat oil over medium-high heat; saute chicken until no longer pink, 4-6 minutes. Remove from pan; keep warm.

2. Add asparagus to skillet; cook and stir over medium-high heat 1 minute. Add garlic; cook and stir 30 seconds. Stir in tomatoes, milk and 2 Tbsp. cheese; cook, covered, over medium heat until cheese begins to melt, 2-3 minutes. Stir in chicken. Serve with rice. If desired, top with additional cheese.

1½ CUPS CHICKEN MIXTURE: 251 cal., 11g fat (3g sat. fat), 74mg chol., 447mg sod., 8g carb. (5g sugars, 3g fiber), 29g pro.

DIABETIC EXCHANGES: 4 lean meat, 2 fat, 1 vegetable.

GRILLED TENDER FLANK STEAK

This marinated steak is so moist that it will become one of your favorite ways to serve beef. You can even prepare it on the grill. It can be easily cut into thin slices.

—Heather Ahrens, Columbus, OH

PREP: 10 MIN. + MARINATING • **COOK:** 20 MIN. • **MAKES:** 6 SERVINGS

- **1 cup reduced-sodium soy sauce**
- **¼ cup lemon juice**
- **¼ cup honey**
- **6 garlic cloves, minced**
- **1 beef flank steak (1½ lbs.)**

SERVE WITH:
Maple-Glazed Green Beans, Page 256

1. In a large shallow bowl, combine the soy sauce, lemon juice, honey and garlic; add steak. Turn to coat; cover and refrigerate for 6-8 hours.

2. Drain and discard marinade. Broil 4-6 in. from the heat or grill over medium heat until meat reaches desired doneness, 8-10 minutes on each side (for medium-rare, a thermometer should read 135°; medium, 140°; medium-well, 145°). Thinly slice steak across the grain.

3 OZ. COOKED BEEF: 186 cal., 8g fat (4g sat. fat), 54mg chol., 471mg sod., 4g carb. (3g sugars, 0 fiber), 23g pro.

DIABETIC EXCHANGES: 3 lean meat.

CRUNCHY-COATED WALLEYE

Potato flakes make a golden coating for these fish fillets, which are a breeze to fry on the stovetop. It's special enough for Sunday dinner but quick enough for busy weeknights.

—Sondra Ostheimer, Boscobel, WI

TAKES: 20 MIN. • **MAKES:** 4 SERVINGS

- **⅓ cup all-purpose flour**
- **1 tsp. paprika**
- **½ tsp. salt**
- **¼ tsp. pepper**
- **¼ tsp. onion powder**
- **¼ tsp. garlic powder**
- **2 large eggs**
- **2¼ lbs. walleye, perch or pike fillets**
- **1½ cups mashed potato flakes**
- **⅓ cup vegetable oil**
- **Tartar sauce and lemon wedges, optional**

1. In a shallow bowl, combine flour, paprika, salt, pepper, onion powder and garlic powder. In another bowl, beat the eggs. Dip both sides of fillets in flour mixture and eggs, then coat with potato flakes.

2. In a large skillet, fry fillets in oil for 5 minutes on each side or until fish flakes easily with a fork. Serve with tartar sauce and lemon if desired.

5 OZ. COOKED FISH: 566 cal., 24g fat (4g sat. fat), 326mg chol., 508mg sod., 29g carb. (0 sugars, 2g fiber), 55g pro.

GRANDMA'S APRON

BY REGINA ROSENBERRY, GREENCASTLE, PENNSYLVANIA

Inside my kitchen drawer is a worn calico apron. The fabric's chocolate background is scattered with blue flowers.

It fits over my shoulders and ties in the back. I wear it with love, for it once hung on a hook in my grandma's kitchen.

In the early mornings, Grandma would don the apron and tie it with a neat little knot at her waist. Her chores awaited as she limped her way to the henhouse and bid good morning to the chickens. After giving them a scoopful of corn, she gathered up the calico hem and nestled several eggs in its large pocket.

Her next stop was the garden, where, sure enough, a handful of beans, a few ripe tomatoes and a yellow squash—to fry in butter for lunch—were waiting to be picked. These treasures joined the eggs in the pocket.

A row of colorful zinnias laughed in the morning sun and spilled from the edge of Grandma's garden. She would stoop to break a few stems, add them to her collection, and then walk back to the house, the screen door slapping behind her.

The day passed as Grandma, still in her apron, performed her tasks of cooking, cleaning and laundering. In the evening after the last dish was washed, the last crumb swept and the last towel folded and tucked away, she'd take off her apron and hang it back on the hook with a sigh.

One morning, Grandma did not appear in the kitchen to slip into her brown and blue calico. Instead, the apron waited on the hook, keeping vigil over the space, which was quiet save for the ticking of the clock. That timepiece ticked away the last few months of Grandma's battle with cancer, before the house stilled and the clock slowly came to a stop.

The apron continued to wait. Peaceful and rested yet somehow lonely.

Months passed before my mother went to Grandma's house to box up her things. She lifted the apron from its hook, and since my grandmother and I share the middle name Elizabeth, Mom presented it to me as a keepsake.

Now the apron is again being filled with fresh eggs. When I walk through my garden, I bunch its hem and load it with warm ripe tomatoes, shiny peppers and thin zucchini. I pluck a few pink zinnias and place them on top of the pile. Memories of Grandma warm my heart as I head back into the house.

At the day's end, I tuck the apron into a drawer and smile. Maybe my young daughter, whose first name is Elizabeth, will someday treasure this simple piece of calico.

I know in my heart of hearts that Grandma would truly be pleased.

For generations, this keepsake in calico has been used to collect eggs, pick zucchini and gather zinnias.

GRANDMA'S SWEDISH MEATBALLS

My mother made these hearty meatballs when we were growing up, and now my kids love them, too. My daughter likes to help toss the meatballs in flour.

—Karin Ness, Big Lake, MN

TAKES: 30 MIN. • **MAKES:** 4 SERVINGS

- **1 large egg, lightly beaten**
- **½ cup crushed saltines (about 10 crackers)**
- **¼ tsp. seasoned salt**
- **¼ tsp. pepper**
- **½ lb. ground beef**
- **½ lb. bulk pork sausage**
- **¼ cup plus 2 Tbsp. all-purpose flour, divided**
- **2½ cups reduced-sodium beef broth, divided**
- **Hot mashed potatoes**
- **Minced fresh parsley, optional**

1. Mix first 4 ingredients. Add the beef and sausage; mix lightly but thoroughly. Shape into 1-in. balls; toss with ¼ cup flour, coating lightly.

2. In a large skillet, brown meatballs over medium-high heat. Add 2 cups broth; bring to a boil. Reduce heat; simmer, covered, until meatballs are cooked through, 5-6 minutes.

3. Remove meatballs with a slotted spoon. Mix the remaining flour and broth until smooth; add to pan. Bring to a boil; cook and stir until thickened, 1-2 minutes. Return meatballs to pan; heat through. Serve with mashed potatoes. If desired, sprinkle with parsley.

1 SERVING: 348 cal., 21g fat (7g sat. fat), 115mg chol., 846mg sod., 17g carb. (1g sugars, 1g fiber), 21g pro.

CHIPOTLE CITRUS-GLAZED TURKEY TENDERLOINS

This simple skillet recipe makes it easy to cook turkey on a weeknight. The combination of sweet, spicy and smoky flavors from orange, peppers and molasses is amazing.

—Darlene Morris, Franklinton, LA

TAKES: 30 MIN. • **MAKES:** 4 SERVINGS (½ CUP SAUCE)

- **4 turkey breast tenderloins (5 oz. each)**
- **¼ tsp. salt**
- **¼ tsp. pepper**
- **1 Tbsp. canola oil**
- **¾ cup orange juice**
- **¼ cup lime juice**
- **¼ cup packed brown sugar**
- **1 Tbsp. molasses**
- **2 tsp. minced chipotle peppers in adobo sauce**
- **2 Tbsp. minced fresh cilantro**

1. Sprinkle turkey with salt and pepper. In a large skillet, brown turkey in oil on all sides.

2. Meanwhile, in a small bowl, whisk the juices, brown sugar, molasses and chipotle peppers; add to skillet. Reduce heat and simmer for 12-16 minutes or until turkey reaches 165°. Transfer turkey to a cutting board; let rest for 5 minutes.

3. Simmer glaze until thickened, about 4 minutes. Slice turkey and serve with glaze. Top with cilantro.

4 OZ. COOKED TURKEY WITH 2 TBSP. GLAZE: 274 cal., 5g fat (0 sat. fat), 56mg chol., 252mg sod., 24g carb. (22g sugars, 0 fiber), 35g pro.

WÜSTHOF

BEEF TENDERLOIN WITH ROASTED VEGETABLES

I appreciate this recipe because it includes a side dish of roasted potatoes, Brussels sprouts and carrots. I prepare it for special dinners throughout the year.

—Janet Singleton, Bellevue, OH

PREP: 20 MIN. + MARINATING • **BAKE:** 1 HOUR + STANDING • **MAKES:** 10 SERVINGS

- **1 beef tenderloin roast (3 lbs.)**
- **¾ cup dry white wine or beef broth**
- **¾ cup reduced-sodium soy sauce**
- **4 tsp. minced fresh rosemary**
- **4 tsp. Dijon mustard**
- **1½ tsp. ground mustard**
- **3 garlic cloves, peeled and sliced**
- **1 lb. Yukon Gold potatoes, cut into 1-in. wedges**
- **1 lb. Brussels sprouts, halved**
- **1 lb. fresh baby carrots**

1. Place tenderloin in a large shallow dish. Combine the wine, soy sauce, rosemary, Dijon mustard, ground mustard and garlic. Pour half of the marinade over tenderloin and turn to coat. Cover and refrigerate for 4-12 hours, turning several times. Cover and refrigerate remaining marinade.

2. Place the potatoes, Brussels sprouts and carrots in a greased 13x9-in. baking dish; add reserved marinade and toss to coat. Cover and bake at 425° for 20 minutes; stir.

3. Drain tenderloin, discarding marinade; if desired, tie tenderloin with baker's twine. Place tenderloin over vegetables. Bake, uncovered, for 40-50 minutes or until meat reaches desired doneness (for medium-rare, a thermometer should read 135°; medium, 140°; medium-well, 145°).

4. Remove beef and let stand for 15 minutes. Check vegetables for doneness. If additional roasting is needed, cover with foil and bake for 10-15 minutes or until tender. Slice beef and serve with vegetables.

1 SERVING: 283 cal., 8g fat (3g sat. fat), 60mg chol., 627mg sod., 16g carb. (4g sugars, 3g fiber), 33g pro.

DIABETIC EXCHANGES: 4 lean meat, 1 vegetable, ½ starch.

PRETZEL-CRUSTED CATFISH

I'm not a big fish lover, so any concoction that has me enjoying fish is a keeper in my book. This combination of flavors works for me. It's awesome served with corn muffins, butter and honey!

—Kelly Williams, Forked River, NJ

TAKES: 30 MIN. • **MAKES:** 4 SERVINGS

- **4 catfish fillets (6 oz. each)**
- **½ tsp. salt**
- **½ tsp. pepper**
- **2 large eggs**
- **⅓ cup Dijon mustard**
- **2 Tbsp. 2% milk**
- **½ cup all-purpose flour**
- **4 cups honey mustard miniature pretzels, coarsely crushed**
- **Oil for frying**
- **Lemon slices, optional**

SERVE WITH:
Smoky Macaroni & Cheese, Page 272

1. Sprinkle catfish with salt and pepper. Whisk eggs, mustard and milk in a shallow bowl. Place flour and pretzels in separate shallow bowls. Coat fillets with flour, then dip in egg mixture and coat with pretzels.

2. Heat ¼ in. oil to 375° in an electric skillet. Fry fillets, a few at a time, until fish flakes easily with a fork, 3-4 minutes on each side. Drain on paper towels. Serve with lemon slices if desired.

1 FILLET: 610 cal., 31g fat (4g sat. fat), 164mg chol., 1579mg sod., 44g carb. (2g sugars, 2g fiber), 33g pro.

SPICED SHORT RIBS

Use your one-pot cooker to make easy work of these tasty short ribs. The recipe is ideal for busy nights when your family wants a big dinner but you are limited on time. The ribs are tender, with the perfect blend of sweet and sour. You can use red wine instead of chicken stock.

—Shanon Tranchina, Massapequa Park, NY

PREP: 20 MIN. • **COOK:** 40 MIN. + RELEASING • **MAKES:** 12 SERVINGS

- **1 Tbsp. olive oil**
- **6 lbs. bone-in beef short ribs**
- **2 Tbsp. butter**
- **1 medium leek (white portion only), finely chopped**
- **1 garlic clove, minced**
- **1 cup chicken stock**
- **1 can (6 oz.) tomato paste**
- **2 Tbsp. ground mustard**
- **2 Tbsp. red wine vinegar**
- **2 Tbsp. Worcestershire sauce**
- **2 tsp. paprika**
- **2 tsp. celery salt**
- **1 tsp. ground cinnamon**
- **½ tsp. pepper**

1. Select saute or browning setting on a 6-qt. electric pressure cooker. Adjust for medium heat; add oil. When oil is hot, brown ribs in batches; set aside.

2. Add butter to pressure cooker. When melted, add leek. Cook and stir leek until tender, 2-3 minutes. Add garlic; cook 1 minute longer. Add stock to pressure cooker. Cook 1 minute, stirring to loosen browned bits from pan. Press cancel.

3. In a small bowl, combine remaining ingredients; spread over ribs. Return ribs to pressure cooker. Lock lid; close pressure-release valve. Adjust to pressure-cook on high for 40 minutes. Let pressure release naturally.

1 SERVING: 232 cal., 14g fat (6g sat. fat), 60mg chol., 324mg sod., 5g carb. (2g sugars, 1g fiber), 20g pro.

TURKEY CURRY WITH RICE

When I have leftover turkey, I make turkey curry with carrots, cauliflower and mango chutney to spoon over rice. It's a special change-of-pace meal any night of the week.

—Nancy Heishman, Las Vegas, NV

TAKES: 30 MIN. • **MAKES:** 6 SERVINGS

1⅓ cups chicken broth
2 Tbsp. curry powder
2 Tbsp. minced fresh cilantro
3 garlic cloves, minced
¾ tsp. salt
½ tsp. ground cardamom
½ tsp. pepper
3 medium carrots, thinly sliced
1 medium onion, finely chopped
1 pkg. (16 oz.) frozen cauliflower, thawed
3 cups chopped cooked turkey
½ cup mango chutney
2 tsp. all-purpose flour
1 cup coconut milk
4½ cups hot cooked rice
Additional mango chutney, optional

1. In a large saucepan, mix the first 7 ingredients. Add carrots and onion; bring to a boil. Reduce heat; simmer, covered, until carrots are crisp-tender, 3-5 minutes. Add cauliflower; cook, covered, until vegetables are tender, 4-6 minutes longer.

2. Stir in turkey and chutney; heat through. In a small bowl, mix flour and coconut milk until smooth; stir into turkey mixture. Bring to a boil, stirring constantly; cook and stir until slightly thickened, 1-2 minutes. Serve with rice and, if desired, additional chutney.

1 CUP TURKEY MIXTURE WITH ¾ CUP RICE: 363 cal., 9g fat (7g sat. fat), 1mg chol., 787mg sod., 64g carb. (16g sugars, 5g fiber), 7g pro.

core

SPICY BEAN & BEEF PIE

My daughter helped me come up with this recipe when we wanted a meal that was different from a casserole. This pie slices nicely and is a comforting and filling dish.

—Debra Dohy, Newcomerstown, OH

PREP: 30 MIN. • BAKE: 30 MIN. • MAKES: 8 SERVINGS

- **1 lb. ground beef**
- **2 to 3 garlic cloves, minced**
- **1 can (11½ oz.) condensed bean with bacon soup, undiluted**
- **1 jar (16 oz.) thick and chunky picante sauce, divided**
- **¼ cup cornstarch**
- **1 Tbsp. chopped fresh parsley**
- **1 tsp. paprika**
- **1 tsp. salt**
- **¼ tsp. pepper**
- **1 can (16 oz.) kidney beans, rinsed and drained**
- **1 can (15 oz.) black beans, rinsed and drained**
- **2 cups shredded cheddar cheese, divided**
- **¾ cup sliced green onions, divided**
- **Dough for double-crust deep-dish pie**
- **1 cup sour cream**
- **1 can (2¼ oz.) sliced ripe olives, drained**

1. Preheat oven to 425°. In a large skillet, cook beef over medium heat until beef is no longer pink. Add garlic; cook 1 minute longer. Drain. In a large bowl, combine soup, 1 cup picante sauce, cornstarch, parsley, paprika, salt and pepper. Fold in beans, 1½ cups cheese, ½ cup onions and beef mixture.

2. On a lightly floured surface, roll half the dough to a ⅛-in.-thick circle; transfer to a 9-in. deep-dish pie plate. Trim even with rim. Add filling. Roll remaining dough to a ⅛-in.-thick circle. Place over filling. Trim, seal and flute edge. Cut slits in top.

3. Bake until crust is lightly browned, 30-35 minutes. Let stand for 5 minutes before cutting. Serve with sour cream, olives and remaining picante sauce, cheese and onions.

FREEZE OPTION: To freeze, before baking, cover and freeze pie for up to 3 months. To use frozen pie: Remove from the freezer 30 minutes before baking. Cover edges of crust loosely with foil; place on a baking sheet. Bake at 425° for 30 minutes. Reduce heat to 350°; remove foil. Bake 55-60 minutes longer or until golden brown. Garnish with sour cream, olives, picante sauce, cheese and onions.

1 PIECE: 931 cal., 56g fat (32g sat. fat), 157mg chol., 1876mg sod., 73g carb. (6g sugars, 9g fiber), 32g pro.

DOUGH FOR A DOUBLE-CRUST DEEP-DISH PIE: Combine 3 cups all-purpose flour and ½ tsp. salt; cut in 1⅓ cups cold butter until crumbly. Gradually add ⅓-¾ cup ice water, tossing with a fork until dough holds together when pressed. Divide dough in half. Shape each into a disk; wrap and refrigerate 1 hour.

APPLE BARBECUE CHICKEN

My husband and I had just moved to Dallas when I first made this recipe. Everything was new—new city, new home—but this dish felt familiar and comforting.

—Darla Andrews, Boerne, TX

TAKES: 30 MIN. • **MAKES:** 6 SERVINGS

- **12 chicken drumsticks**
- **¼ tsp. pepper**
- **1 Tbsp. olive oil**
- **1 bottle (18 oz.) sweet and spicy barbecue sauce**
- **2 cups applesauce**
- **⅓ cup packed brown sugar**
- **1 Tbsp. chili powder**

1. Sprinkle drumsticks with pepper. In a Dutch oven, heat oil over medium heat. Brown drumsticks in batches; drain. Remove from pan.

2. Add remaining ingredients to pan, stirring to combine. Return chicken to pan; bring to a boil. Reduce heat; simmer, covered, 20-25 minutes or until chicken is tender.

2 CHICKEN DRUMSTICKS WITH ½ CUP SAUCE: 501 cal., 15g fat (4g sat. fat), 95mg chol., 949mg sod., 58g carb. (50g sugars, 1g fiber), 29g pro.

CIDER-GLAZED HAM

Here is a heartwarming and classic way to serve ham. Apple cider and mustard perfectly accent the ham's rich, smoky flavor.

—Jennifer Foos-Furer, Marysville, OH

PREP: 15 MIN. • **COOK:** 4 HOURS • **MAKES:** 8 SERVINGS

- **1 boneless fully cooked ham (3 lbs.)**
- **1¾ cups apple cider or juice**
- **¼ cup packed brown sugar**
- **¼ cup Dijon mustard**
- **¼ cup honey**
- **2 Tbsp. cornstarch**
- **2 Tbsp. cold water**

1. Place ham in a 5-qt. slow cooker. In a small bowl, combine the cider, brown sugar, mustard and honey; pour over ham. Cover and cook on low for 4-5 hours or until heated through. Remove ham and keep warm.

2. Pour cooking juices into a small saucepan. Combine cornstarch and water until smooth; stir into cooking juices. Bring to a boil; cook and stir for 2 minutes or until thickened. Serve with ham.

4 OZ. COOKED HAM WITH ABOUT ¼ CUP GLAZE: 280 cal., 6g fat (2g sat. fat), 86mg chol., 1954mg sod., 26g carb. (21g sugars, 0 fiber), 31g pro.

CHICKEN-STUFFED CUBANELLE PEPPERS

Here's a new take on traditional stuffed peppers. I substituted chicken for the beef and used Cubanelle peppers in place of the usual green peppers.

—Bev Burlingame, Canton, OH

PREP: 20 MIN. • **BAKE:** 1 HOUR • **MAKES:** 6 SERVINGS

- **6 Cubanelle peppers or mild banana peppers**
- **2 large eggs, lightly beaten**
- **3 cups shredded cooked chicken breast**
- **1 cup salsa**
- **¾ cup soft bread crumbs**
- **½ cup cooked long grain rice**
- **2 cups meatless pasta sauce**

1. Preheat oven to 350°. Cut and discard tops from peppers; remove seeds. In a large bowl, mix eggs, chicken, salsa, bread crumbs and rice. Spoon into peppers.

2. Spread pasta sauce onto bottom of a 13x9-in. baking dish coated with cooking spray. Top with peppers. Bake, covered, 60-65 minutes or until peppers are tender and a thermometer inserted in stuffing reads at least 165°.

1 STUFFED PEPPER: 230 cal., 4g fat (1g sat. fat), 125mg chol., 661mg sod., 20g carb. (7g sugars, 5g fiber), 26g pro.

DIABETIC EXCHANGES: 3 lean meat, 2 vegetable, 1 starch.

SLOW-COOKED BEEF BRISKET

One bite of this super tender brisket, and your family will be hooked! The rich gravy is perfect for spooning over a side of creamy mashed potatoes.

—Eunice Stoen, Decorah, IA

PREP: 15 MIN. • **COOK:** 8 HOURS • **MAKES:** 6 SERVINGS

- **1 fresh beef brisket (2½ to 3 lbs.)**
- **2 tsp. liquid smoke, optional**
- **1 tsp. celery salt**
- **½ tsp. pepper**
- **¼ tsp. salt**
- **1 large onion, sliced**
- **1 can (12 oz.) beer or nonalcoholic beer**
- **2 tsp. Worcestershire sauce**
- **2 Tbsp. cornstarch**
- **¼ cup cold water**

1. Cut brisket in half; rub with liquid smoke, if desired, and celery salt, pepper and salt. Place in a 3-qt. slow cooker. Top with onion. Combine beer and Worcestershire sauce; pour over meat. Cover and cook on low for 8-9 hours or until tender.

2. Remove brisket and keep warm. Strain cooking juices; transfer to a small saucepan. In a small bowl, combine cornstarch and water until smooth; stir into juices. Bring to a boil; cook and stir until thickened, about 2 minutes. Serve beef with gravy.

5 OZ. COOKED BRISKET WITH ABOUT ⅓ CUP SAUCE: 285 cal., 8g fat (3g sat. fat), 80mg chol., 430mg sod., 7g carb. (3g sugars, 0 fiber), 39g pro.

DIABETIC EXCHANGES: 5 lean meat, ½ starch.

APPLE ROASTED PORK WITH CHERRY BALSAMIC GLAZE

I added roasted apples, cherries and onions to turn ordinary pork into a sensational dish and haven't turned back since. There's a short time frame between caramelized onions and burned ones, so pay close attention once they start cooking.

—Josh Downey, Mchenry, IL

PREP: 30 MIN. • **BAKE:** 50 MIN+ STANDING • **MAKES:** 8 SERVINGS

- **1 boneless pork loin roast (3 lbs.)**
- **1½ tsp. salt, divided**
- **¾ tsp. pepper, divided**
- **¼ cup olive oil, divided**
- **3 medium apples, sliced**
- **1½ cups unsweetened apple juice**
- **6 medium onions, sliced (about 5 cups)**
- **3 Tbsp. balsamic vinegar**
- **1½ cups frozen pitted dark sweet cherries**
- **½ cup cherry juice**

1. Preheat oven to 350°. Sprinkle roast with 1 tsp. salt and ½ tsp. pepper. In an ovenproof Dutch oven, heat 2 Tbsp. oil over medium-high heat; brown roast on all sides. Add apples and apple juice to pan. Bake, uncovered, 50-60 minutes or until a thermometer inserted in pork reads 145°, basting occasionally with pan juices.

2. Meanwhile, in a large skillet, heat remaining oil over medium heat. Add onions and the remaining salt and pepper; cook and stir 8-10 minutes or until softened. Reduce heat to medium-low. Cook 35-40 minutes or until deep golden brown, stirring occasionally. Keep warm.

3. Remove roast and apples to a serving plate; tent with foil. Let roast stand 10 minutes before slicing.

4. Skim fat from pork pan juices. Place over medium-high heat; add vinegar and cook 1 minute, stirring to loosen browned bits from pan. Stir in cherries and cherry juice. Bring to a boil; cook 10-15 minutes or until mixture is reduced to about 1 cup. Serve pork, apples and onions with cherry glaze.

1 SERVING: 387 cal., 15g fat (4g sat. fat), 85mg chol., 498mg sod., 29g carb. (20g sugars, 3g fiber), 34g pro.

AUTUMN APPLE CHICKEN

I'd just been apple picking and wanted to bake something new with the bounty. Slow-cooking chicken with apples and barbecue sauce filled my whole house with the most delicious smell. We couldn't wait to eat.

—Caitlyn Hauser, Brookline, NH

PREP: 20 MIN. • **COOK:** 3½ HOURS • **MAKES:** 4 SERVINGS

- **1 Tbsp. canola oil**
- **4 bone-in chicken thighs (about 1½ lbs.), skin removed**
- **¼ tsp. salt**
- **¼ tsp. pepper**
- **2 medium Fuji or Gala apples, coarsely chopped**
- **1 medium onion, chopped**
- **1 garlic clove, minced**
- **⅓ cup barbecue sauce**
- **¼ cup apple cider or juice**
- **1 Tbsp. honey**

1. In a large skillet, heat oil over medium heat. Brown chicken thighs on both sides; sprinkle with salt and pepper. Transfer to a 3-qt. slow cooker; top with apples.

2. Add onion to same skillet; cook and stir over medium heat 2-3 minutes or until tender. Add garlic; cook 1 minute longer. Stir in barbecue sauce, apple cider and honey; increase heat to medium-high. Cook 1 minute, stirring to loosen browned bits from pan. Pour over chicken and apples. Cook, covered, on low 3½-4½ hours or until chicken is tender.

FREEZE OPTION: Freeze cooled chicken mixture in freezer containers. To use, partially thaw in refrigerator overnight. Heat through in a covered saucepan, stirring occasionally.

1 CHICKEN THIGH WITH ½ CUP APPLE MIXTURE: 333 cal., 13g fat (3g sat. fat), 87mg chol., 456mg sod., 29g carb. (22g sugars, 3g fiber), 25g pro.

DIABETIC EXCHANGES: 4 lean meat, 1½ starch, ½ fruit.

GRILLED ROAST BEEF

A simple dry rub is enough to turn roast beef into a real crowd-pleaser. The slightly spicy meat is irresistible as is, and as leftovers, piled on top of fresh, crusty bread.

—Allison Ector, Ardmore, PA

PREP: 20 MIN. + CHILLING • **GRILL:** 1 HOUR + STANDING • **MAKES:** 6 SERVINGS

- **4 Tbsp. paprika**
- **3 Tbsp. brown sugar**
- **2 Tbsp. chili powder**
- **1 Tbsp. garlic powder**
- **1 Tbsp. white pepper**
- **1 Tbsp. celery salt**
- **1 Tbsp. ground cumin**
- **1 Tbsp. dried oregano**
- **1 Tbsp. pepper**
- **2 tsp. cayenne pepper**
- **1 tsp. ground mustard**
- **1 beef tri-tip roast or beef sirloin tip roast (2 to 3 lbs.)**
- **2 cups soaked hickory wood chips or chunks**
- **2 Tbsp. canola oil**

1. Combine the first 11 ingredients; rub desired amount over roast. Wrap and refrigerate overnight. Store leftover dry rub in an airtight container for up to 6 months.

2. Remove roast from the refrigerator 1 hour before grilling. Prepare grill for indirect heat, using a drip pan. Add wood chips according to manufacturer's directions.

3. Unwrap roast and brush with oil; place over drip pan. Grill, covered, over medium-low indirect heat for 1-1½ hours or until meat reaches desired doneness (for medium-rare, a thermometer should read 135°; medium, 140°; medium-well, 145°). Let stand for 10-15 minutes before slicing.

4 OZ. COOKED BEEF: 294 cal., 16g fat (4g sat. fat), 91mg chol., 324mg sod., 5g carb. (3g sugars, 1g fiber), 32g pro.

DIABETIC EXCHANGES: 4 lean meat, 1 fat.

BAKED ROAST BEEF: Prepare roast and refrigerate as directed. Unwrap roast and brush with oil and ½ tsp. liquid smoke. Place on a rack in a shallow roasting pan. Bake, uncovered, at 425° for 55-75 minutes or until meat reaches desired doneness.

APPLE & WALNUT STUFFED PORK TENDERLOIN WITH RED CURRANT SAUCE

My roasted pork tenderloin is stuffed with two of our favorite ingredients: walnuts and apples. This comforting entree is my family's most requested pork dish.

—Gloria Bradley, Naperville, IL

PREP: 35 MIN. • **BAKE:** 55 MIN. • **MAKES:** 6 SERVINGS

- **1 Tbsp. butter**
- **1 cup chopped walnuts**
- **1 medium apple, peeled and finely chopped**
- **3 Tbsp. dried cranberries**
- **1 Tbsp. minced fresh parsley**
- **1 Tbsp. olive oil**
- **1 garlic clove, minced**
- **1 pork tenderloin (1½ lbs.)**
- **⅓ cup apple butter**
- **½ tsp. salt**
- **½ tsp. ground coriander**

SAUCE

- **1 cup red currant jelly**
- **1 shallot, finely chopped**
- **2 Tbsp. cranberry juice**
- **2 Tbsp. honey**
- **1 Tbsp. dried currants**
- **1 Tbsp. cider vinegar**

1. In a large heavy skillet, melt butter. Add walnuts; cook and stir over medium heat until toasted, about 2 minutes. Remove ½ cup for serving. Add apple to the remaining walnuts; cook and stir 1 minute longer. Cool slightly.

2. Place the cranberries, parsley, oil, garlic and apple mixture in a food processor; cover and process until finely chopped.

3. Cut a lengthwise slit down the center of the roast to within ½ in. of bottom. Open roast so it lies flat; cover with plastic wrap. Flatten to ½-in. thickness. Remove wrap; spread apple butter on 1 long side of tenderloin to within ¼ in. of edges. Top with apple mixture. Close meat; tie with kitchen string. Place on a rack in a shallow roasting pan; rub with salt and coriander.

4. Bake at 350° until a thermometer inserted into the center of the stuffing reads 165° and thermometer inserted in the pork reads at least 145°, 55-65 minutes. Let stand at least 10 minutes before slicing.

5. Meanwhile, in a small saucepan, combine sauce ingredients; bring to a boil. Reduce heat; simmer, uncovered, until slightly thickened, 12-14 minutes. Serve with the pork; top with the reserved walnuts.

3 OZ. COOKED PORK WITH 3 TBSP. SAUCE: 513 cal., 21g fat (4g sat. fat), 68mg chol., 260mg sod., 59g carb. (51g sugars, 2g fiber), 26g pro.

CITRUS-HERB ROAST CHICKEN

This dish is one of my all-time favorites. The flavorful, juicy chicken combines with the aromas of spring in fresh herbs, lemon and onions to form the perfect one-pot meal. I make the gravy right in the pan.

—Megan Fordyce, Fairchance, PA

PREP: 25 MIN. • **BAKE:** 2 HOURS + STANDING • **MAKES:** 8 SERVINGS

- **6 garlic cloves**
- **1 roasting chicken (6 to 7 lbs.)**
- **3 lbs. baby red potatoes, halved**
- **6 medium carrots, halved lengthwise and cut into 1-in. pieces**
- **4 fresh thyme sprigs**
- **4 fresh dill sprigs**
- **2 fresh rosemary sprigs**
- **1 medium lemon**
- **1 small navel orange**
- **1 tsp. salt**
- **½ tsp. pepper**
- **3 cups chicken broth, warmed**
- **6 green onions, cut into 2-in. pieces**

1. Preheat oven to 350°. Peel and cut garlic into quarters. Place chicken on a cutting board. Tuck wings under chicken. With a sharp paring knife, cut 24 small slits in breasts, drumsticks and thighs. Insert garlic in slits. Tie drumsticks together.

2. Place potatoes and carrots in a shallow roasting pan; top with herbs. Place chicken, breast side up, over vegetables and herbs. Cut lemon and orange in half; gently squeeze the juices over chicken and vegetables. Place squeezed fruits inside chicken cavity. Sprinkle chicken with salt and pepper. Pour broth around the chicken.

3. Roast until a thermometer inserted in thickest part of thigh reads 170°-175°, 2-2½ hours, sprinkling green onions over vegetables during the last 20 minutes. (Cover loosely with foil if chicken browns too quickly.)

4. Remove chicken from oven; tent with foil. Let stand for 15 minutes before carving. Discard herbs. If desired, skim fat and thicken pan drippings for gravy. Serve gravy with chicken and vegetables.

7 OZ. COOKED CHICKEN WITH 1¼ CUPS VEGETABLES: 561 cal., 24g fat (7g sat. fat), 136mg chol., 826mg sod., 39g carb. (5g sugars, 5g fiber), 47g pro.

LE CREUSET

MEATBALL CHILI WITH DUMPLINGS

My family enjoys this delicious recipe—it's like a spicy meatball stew with dumplings!

—Sarah Yoder, Middlebury, IN

PREP: 20 MIN. • **COOK:** 50 MIN. • **MAKES:** 6 SERVINGS

- **1 large egg, beaten**
- **¾ cup finely chopped onion, divided**
- **¼ cup dry bread crumbs or rolled oats**
- **5 tsp. beef bouillon granules, divided**
- **3 tsp. chili powder, divided**
- **1 lb. ground beef**
- **3 Tbsp. all-purpose flour**
- **1 Tbsp. canola oil**
- **1 can (28 oz.) diced tomatoes, undrained**
- **1 garlic clove, minced**
- **½ tsp. ground cumin**
- **1 can (16 oz.) kidney beans, rinsed and drained**

CORNMEAL DUMPLINGS

- **1½ cups biscuit/baking mix**
- **½ cup yellow cornmeal**
- **⅔ cup 2% milk**
- **Minced chives, optional**

1. In a large bowl, combine egg, ¼ cup onion, bread crumbs, 3 tsp. bouillon and 1 tsp. chili powder; crumble beef over mixture and mix lightly but thoroughly. Shape into twelve 1½-in. meatballs. Roll in flour.

2. Heat oil in a 12-in. cast-iron or other ovenproof skillet; brown meatballs. Drain on paper towels. Wipe skillet clean with paper towels. Add tomatoes, garlic, cumin and the remaining onion, bouillon and chili powder to skillet; stir to combine. Add the meatballs. Cover and cook over low heat about 20 minutes. Stir in beans.

3. Combine dumpling ingredients. Drop by spoonfuls onto chili; cook on low, uncovered, for 10 minutes. Cover and cook until a toothpick inserted in dumpling comes out clean, 10-12 minutes longer. If desired, sprinkle with minced chives.

1 SERVING: 475 cal., 16g fat (6g sat. fat), 76mg chol., 1523mg sod., 56g carb. (8g sugars, 7g fiber), 26g pro.

PEACH-GLAZED RIBS

For a mouthwatering alternative to the usual barbecue sauce for ribs, try this slightly spicy recipe. The peaches add just the right touch of sweetness and a lovely color to this special sauce.

—Sharon Taylor, Columbia, SC

PREP: 15 MIN. • **GRILL:** 1¼ HOURS • **MAKES:** 6 SERVINGS

- **3 to 4 lbs. pork baby back ribs, cut into serving-size pieces**
- **1 can (15¼ oz.) peach halves, drained**
- **⅓ cup soy sauce**
- **¼ cup canola oil**
- **¼ cup honey**
- **2 Tbsp. brown sugar**
- **1 tsp. sesame seeds, toasted**
- **1 garlic clove, peeled**
- **¼ tsp. ground ginger**

SERVE WITH: Emily's Honey Lime Coleslaw, Page 235

1. Prepare grill for indirect heat, using a drip pan. Place ribs over drip pan. Grill, covered, over indirect medium heat for 60 minutes, turning occasionally.

2. Meanwhile, in a blender, combine the remaining ingredients; cover and process until smooth. Baste ribs.

3. Grill until meat is tender and juices run clear, 15-20 minutes longer, basting occasionally with remaining sauce.

1 SERVING: 568 cal., 40g fat (13g sat. fat), 122mg chol., 930mg sod., 25g carb. (23g sugars, 1g fiber), 28g pro.

GRILLED RIBEYES WITH BROWNED GARLIC BUTTER

Use the grill's smoke to flavor ribeyes, then slather them with garlicky butter for a standout entree your family will always remember.

—Arge Salvatori, Waldwick, NJ

TAKES: 25 MIN. • **MAKES:** 8 SERVINGS

- **6 Tbsp. unsalted butter, cubed**
- **2 garlic cloves, minced**
- **4 beef ribeye steaks (about 1 in. thick and 12 oz. each)**
- **1½ tsp. salt**
- **1½ tsp. pepper**

1. In a small heavy saucepan, melt the butter with garlic over medium heat. Heat 4-6 minutes or until butter is golden brown, stirring constantly. Remove from heat.

2. Season the steaks with salt and pepper. Grill, covered, over medium heat or broil 4 in. from heat 5-7 minutes on each side or until meat reaches desired doneness (for medium-rare, a meat thermometer should read 135°; medium, 140°; medium-well, 145°).

3. Gently warm garlic butter over low heat. Serve with steaks.

4 OZ. COOKED BEEF WITH 2 TSP. GARLIC BUTTER: 449 cal., 36g fat (16g sat. fat), 123mg chol., 521mg sod., 1g carb. (0 sugars, 0 fiber), 30g pro.

COUNTRY-FRIED STEAK

A healthier country-fried steak? Sounds like an oxymoron, but it's not. This family favorite keeps its classic comfort-food flavor while dropping over half the fat.

—Taste of Home *Test Kitchen*

PREP: 20 MIN. • **COOK:** 15 MIN. • **MAKES:** 4 SERVINGS

- **1 beef top round steak (1 lb.)**
- **½ tsp. salt**
- **½ tsp. garlic powder, divided**
- **½ tsp. pepper, divided**
- **¼ tsp. onion powder**
- **½ cup buttermilk**
- **¾ cup plus 4½ tsp. all-purpose flour, divided**
- **1 Tbsp. canola oil**
- **4½ tsp. butter**
- **1 cup 2% milk**

1. Cut steak into 4 serving-size pieces; pound to ¼-in. thickness. Combine the salt, ¼ tsp. garlic powder, ¼ tsp. pepper and onion powder; sprinkle over steaks.

2. Place buttermilk and ¾ cup flour in separate shallow bowls. Dip steaks in buttermilk, then flour.

3. In a large skillet, cook steaks in oil over medium heat until meat is no longer pink, 3-4 minutes on each side. Remove and keep warm.

4. In a small saucepan, melt butter. Stir in remaining flour until smooth; gradually add milk. Bring to a boil; cook and stir until thickened, about 1 minute. Stir in remaining garlic powder and pepper. Serve with steak.

1 PIECE WITH ¼ CUP GRAVY: 318 cal., 13g fat (5g sat. fat), 80mg chol., 410mg sod., 19g carb. (4g sugars, 1g fiber), 30g pro.

WHITE SEAFOOD LASAGNA

We make lasagna with shrimp and scallops as part of an Italian feast.

—Joe Colamonico, North Charleston, SC

PREP: 1 HOUR • **BAKE:** 40 MIN. + STANDING • **MAKES:** 12 SERVINGS

- **9 uncooked lasagna noodles**
- **1 Tbsp. butter**
- **1 lb. uncooked shrimp (31 to 40 per lb.), peeled and deveined**
- **1 lb. bay scallops**
- **5 garlic cloves, minced**
- **¼ cup white wine**
- **1 Tbsp. lemon juice**
- **1 lb. fresh crabmeat**

CHEESE SAUCE

- **¼ cup butter, cubed**
- **¼ cup all-purpose flour**
- **3 cups 2% milk**
- **1 cup shredded part-skim mozzarella cheese**
- **½ cup grated Parmesan cheese**
- **½ tsp. salt**
- **¼ tsp. pepper**
- **Dash ground nutmeg**

RICOTTA MIXTURE

- **1 carton (15 oz.) part-skim ricotta cheese**
- **1 pkg. (10 oz.) frozen chopped spinach, thawed and squeezed dry**
- **1 cup shredded part-skim mozzarella cheese**
- **½ cup grated Parmesan cheese**
- **½ cup seasoned bread crumbs**
- **1 large egg, lightly beaten**

TOPPING

- **1 cup shredded part-skim mozzarella cheese**
- **¼ cup grated Parmesan cheese**
- **Minced fresh parsley**

1. Preheat oven to 350°. Cook lasagna noodles according to package directions; drain.

2. Meanwhile, in a large skillet, heat butter over medium heat. Add shrimp and scallops in batches; cook 2-4 minutes or until shrimp turn pink and scallops are firm and opaque. Remove from pan.

3. Add garlic to same pan; cook 1 minute. Add wine and lemon juice, stirring to loosen browned bits from pan. Bring to a boil; cook 1-2 minutes or until liquid is reduced by half. Add crab; heat through. Stir in shrimp and scallops.

4. For cheese sauce, melt butter over medium heat in a large saucepan. Stir in flour until smooth; gradually whisk in milk. Bring to a boil, stirring constantly; cook and stir until thickened, 1-2 minutes. Remove from heat; stir in remaining cheese sauce ingredients. In a large bowl, combine ingredients for ricotta mixture; stir in 1 cup cheese sauce.

5. Spread ½ cup cheese sauce into a greased 13x9-in. baking dish. Layer with 3 noodles, half of the ricotta mixture, half of the seafood mixture and ⅔ cup cheese sauce. Repeat layers. Top with remaining noodles and cheese sauce. Sprinkle top with 1 cup mozzarella cheese and ¼ cup Parmesan cheese.

6. Bake, uncovered, 40-50 minutes or until casserole is bubbly and top is golden brown. Let stand 10 minutes before serving. Sprinkle with parsley.

1 PIECE: 448 cal., 19g fat (11g sat. fat), 158mg chol., 957mg sod., 29g carb. (5g sugars, 2g fiber), 39g pro.

CHAPTER 4

COUNTRY SIDES, SALADS & MORE

From garden-fresh salads and harvesttime sides to buttery breads and heartwarming soups, the farmhouse recipes found here make for a chapter you'll turn to time and again.

SIMPLE AU GRATIN POTATOES

These cheesy potatoes are always welcome at our dinner table, and they're so simple to make. A perfect complement to ham, this versatile, homey side dish also goes well with pork, chicken and other entrees.

—Cris O'Brien, Virginia Beach, VA

PREP: 20 MIN. • **BAKE:** 1½ HOURS • **MAKES:** 8 SERVINGS

- **3 Tbsp. butter**
- **3 Tbsp. all-purpose flour**
- **1½ tsp. salt**
- **⅛ tsp. pepper**
- **2 cups 2% milk**
- **1 cup shredded cheddar cheese**
- **5 cups thinly sliced peeled potatoes (about 6 medium)**
- **½ cup chopped onion**
- **Additional pepper, optional**

1. Preheat oven to 350°. In a large saucepan, melt butter over low heat. Stir in flour, salt and pepper until smooth. Gradually add milk. Bring to a boil; cook and stir 2 minutes or until thickened. Remove from heat; stir in cheese until melted. Add potatoes and onion.

2. Transfer to a greased 2-qt. baking dish. Cover and bake 1 hour. Uncover; bake 30-40 minutes or until the potatoes are tender. If desired, top with additional pepper.

¾ CUP: 224 cal., 10g fat (7g sat. fat), 35mg chol., 605mg sod., 26g carb. (4g sugars, 2g fiber), 7g pro.

RIBBON SALAD WITH ORANGE VINAIGRETTE

Zucchini, cucumbers and carrots are peeled into ribbons for this citrusy salad. We like to serve it for parties and special occasions.

—Nancy Heishman, Las Vegas, NV

TAKES: 30 MIN. • **MAKES:** 8 SERVINGS

- **1 medium zucchini**
- **1 medium cucumber**
- **1 medium carrot**
- **3 medium oranges**
- **3 cups fresh baby spinach**
- **4 green onions, finely chopped**
- **½ cup chopped walnuts**
- **½ tsp. salt**
- **½ tsp. pepper**
- **½ cup golden raisins, optional**

VINAIGRETTE

- **¼ cup olive oil**
- **4 tsp. white wine vinegar**
- **1 Tbsp. finely chopped green onion**
- **2 tsp. honey**
- **¼ tsp. salt**
- **¼ tsp. pepper**

1. Using a vegetable peeler, shave zucchini, cucumber and carrot lengthwise into very thin strips.

2. Finely grate enough zest from oranges to measure 2 Tbsp. Cut 1 orange crosswise in half; squeeze juice from orange to measure ½ cup. Reserve zest and juice for vinaigrette. Cut a thin slice from the top and bottom of remaining oranges; stand oranges upright on a cutting board. With a knife, cut off peel and outer membrane from orange. Cut along the membrane of each segment to remove fruit.

3. In a large bowl, combine spinach, orange sections, green onions, walnuts, salt, pepper and, if desired, raisins. Add vegetable ribbons; gently toss to combine. In a small bowl, combine vinaigrette ingredients. Add reserved orange zest and juice; whisk until blended. Drizzle half of the vinaigrette over salad; toss to coat. Serve with remaining vinaigrette.

1½ CUPS: 162 cal., 12g fat (1g sat. fat), 0 chol., 240mg sod., 14g carb. (9g sugars, 2g fiber), 3g pro.

DIABETIC EXCHANGES: 2 fat, 1 vegetable, ½ starch.

GIVING FROM THE FAMILY GARDEN

BY KARIE CHATHAM, MOUNT OLIVE, MISSISSIPPI

Growing up, I'd never heard the term "community garden." I suppose it's more common in larger cities, where a garden at home is not always possible, but the benefits of a community garden are vast—and in a way, thanks to my grandparents, I've had one all my life.

My brother and I grew up picking corn and peas in the early summer mornings on my grandparents' farm, when school was out and our parents worked during the day. We would pick and then pile all of our produce into 5-gallon buckets at the end of the rows.

Neighbors would often drive up and talk to Grandpa from their cars, and he always offered them corn or peas or whatever else we were picking. I couldn't believe it—we had worked so hard on it! But as I grew older, I realized that giving food was better than a store-bought gift. Food takes time, money and patience. It's a gift with love behind it.

My grandparents are the most giving people I know. I started sixth grade just before Hurricane Katrina hit in 2005. My family, extended and immediate, all waited out the storm together. Power was out and businesses closed for a while, so I spent time off school with my family. My grandfather donated supplies to people in town from the back of a truck, and my brother and I helped Grandpa hand them out.

During the rebuilding, my grandmother once cooked all of our frozen vegetables and meat, loaded it all up in the back of her vehicle, and drove to where utility workers were repairing power lines. People had come from all over the country to help out, and she was determined to feed at least some of them. Once again, my brother and I helped. We drove up, popped open

Grandpa (left and above) taught Karie (above) the joy of sharing homegrown food with the community.

the trunk and got to work. That day, we served complete strangers home-cooked meals from the pots and pans in Grandma's car.

A garden is wonderful, but a community is what makes the scorching sun, the sweat and the bending over worthwhile. I hope people in cities are able to grow their own food, whether in backyards or a community garden alongside neighbors, because connection and food sharing are what make having a garden special. I'm lucky to have had something like it my entire life.

RED & GREEN SALAD WITH TOASTED ALMONDS

During a long Midwest winter, I crave greens and tomatoes from the garden. This salad has a fantastic out-of-the-garden taste. Thank goodness I can get the ingredients all year-round.

—Jasmine Rose, Crystal Lake, IL

TAKES: 25 MIN. • **MAKES:** 12 SERVINGS

- **¼ cup red wine vinegar**
- **1 Tbsp. reduced-sodium soy sauce**
- **2 garlic cloves, minced**
- **2 tsp. sesame oil**
- **2 tsp. honey**
- **1 tsp. minced fresh gingerroot or ½ tsp. ground ginger**
- **⅛ tsp. Louisiana-style hot sauce**
- **½ cup grapeseed or canola oil**

SALAD

- **2 heads Boston or Bibb lettuce, torn**
- **1 head red leaf lettuce**
- **1 medium sweet red pepper, julienned**
- **2 celery ribs, sliced**
- **1 cup sliced English cucumber**
- **1 cup frozen peas, thawed**
- **1 cup grape tomatoes, halved**
- **1 cup sliced almonds, toasted**

1. In a small bowl, whisk the first 7 ingredients. Gradually whisk in grapeseed oil until blended.

2. In a large bowl, combine lettuces, red pepper, celery, cucumber, peas and tomatoes. Just before serving, pour dressing over salad and toss to coat. Sprinkle with almonds.

1⅓ CUPS: 168 cal., 14g fat (1g sat. fat), 0 chol., 90mg sod., 8g carb. (3g sugars, 3g fiber), 4g pro.

DIABETIC EXCHANGES: 3 fat, 1 vegetable.

DUTCH-OVEN BREAD

Crackling homemade bread makes an average day extraordinary. Enjoy this beautiful crusty bread recipe as is, or stir in a few favorites like cheese, garlic, herbs and dried fruits.

—Catherine Ward, Mequon, WI

PREP: 15 MIN. + RISING • **BAKE:** 45 MIN. + COOLING • **MAKES:** 1 LOAF (16 SLICES)

- **3 to 3½ cups (125 grams per cup) all-purpose flour**
- **1 tsp. active dry yeast**
- **1 tsp. salt**
- **1½ cups water (70° to 75°)**

1. In a large bowl, whisk 3 cups flour, yeast and salt. Stir in water and enough remaining flour to form a moist, shaggy dough. Do not knead. Cover and let rise in a cool place until doubled, 7-8 hours.

2. Preheat oven to 450°; place a Dutch oven with lid onto center rack and heat for at least 30 minutes. Once Dutch oven is heated, turn dough onto a generously floured surface. Using a metal scraper or spatula, quickly shape into a round loaf. Gently place on top of a piece of parchment.

3. Using a sharp knife, make a slash (¼ in. deep) across top of loaf. Using the parchment, immediately lower bread into heated Dutch oven. Cover; bake for 30 minutes. Uncover and bake until bread is deep golden brown and sounds hollow when tapped, 15-20 minutes longer, partially covering if browning too much. Remove loaf from pan and cool completely on wire rack.

1 SLICE: 86 cal., 0 fat (0 sat. fat), 0 chol., 148mg sod., 18g carb. (0 sugars, 1g fiber), 3g pro.

CREAMY ROOT VEGGIE SOUP

On chilly nights, we fill the pot with parsnips and celery root for a smooth, creamy soup. Garlic, bacon and fresh thyme make it even better.

—Sally Sibthorpe, Shelby Township, MI

PREP: 15 MIN. • **COOK:** 1 HOUR • **MAKES:** 8 SERVINGS

- **4 bacon strips, chopped**
- **1 large onion, chopped**
- **3 garlic cloves, minced**
- **1 large celery root, peeled and cubed (about 5 cups)**
- **6 medium parsnips, peeled and cubed (about 4 cups)**
- **6 cups chicken stock**
- **1 bay leaf**
- **1 cup heavy whipping cream**
- **2 tsp. minced fresh thyme**
- **1 tsp. salt**
- **¼ tsp. white pepper**
- **¼ tsp. ground nutmeg**
- **Additional minced fresh thyme**

1. In a Dutch oven, cook bacon over medium heat until crisp, stirring occasionally. Remove with a slotted spoon; drain on paper towels. Cook and stir onion in bacon drippings about 6-8 minutes or until tender. Add garlic; cook 1 minute longer.

2. Add celery root, parsnips, stock and bay leaf. Bring to a boil. Reduce heat; cook, uncovered, for 30-40 minutes or until the vegetables are tender. Remove bay leaf.

3. Puree soup using an immersion blender. Or, cool slightly and puree in batches in a blender; return to pan. Stir in cream, 2 tsp. thyme, salt, pepper and nutmeg; heat through. Top servings with bacon and additional thyme.

1 CUP: 295 cal., 17g fat (9g sat. fat), 50mg chol., 851mg sod., 30g carb. (9g sugars, 6g fiber), 8g pro.

MOM'S SWEET POTATO BAKE

Mom loves sweet potatoes and fixed them often in this creamy, comforting casserole. With its nutty topping, this side dish could almost serve as a dessert. It's a treat!

—Sandi Pichon, Memphis, TN

PREP: 10 MIN. • **BAKE:** 45 MIN. • **MAKES:** 8 SERVINGS

3 cups cold mashed sweet potatoes (prepared without milk or butter)
1 cup sugar
3 large eggs
½ cup 2% milk
¼ cup butter, softened
1 tsp. salt
1 tsp. vanilla extract

TOPPING

½ cup packed brown sugar
½ cup chopped pecans
¼ cup all-purpose flour
2 Tbsp. cold butter

1. Preheat oven to 325°. In a large bowl, beat sweet potatoes, sugar, eggs, milk, butter, salt and vanilla until smooth. Transfer to a greased 2-qt. baking dish.

2. In a small bowl, combine the brown sugar, pecans and flour; cut in butter until crumbly. Sprinkle over the sweet potato mixture. Bake, uncovered, until a thermometer reads 160°, 45-50 minutes.

½ CUP: 417 cal., 16g fat (7g sat. fat), 94mg chol., 435mg sod., 65g carb. (47g sugars, 4g fiber), 6g pro.

HERB QUICK BREAD

This simple bread is especially good with soups and stews, but slices are also tasty alongside fresh, green salads. The herbs make it a flavorful treat for Sunday dinners.

—Donna Roberts, Manhattan, KS

PREP: 15 MIN. • **BAKE:** 40 MIN. + COOLING • **MAKES:** 1 LOAF (16 SLICES)

- **3 cups all-purpose flour**
- **3 Tbsp. sugar**
- **1 Tbsp. baking powder**
- **3 tsp. caraway seeds**
- **½ tsp. salt**
- **½ tsp. ground nutmeg**
- **½ tsp. dried thyme**
- **1 large egg, room temperature**
- **1 cup fat-free milk**
- **⅓ cup canola oil**

1. Preheat oven to 350°. In a large bowl, whisk together first 7 ingredients. In another bowl, whisk together egg, milk and oil. Add to flour mixture; stir just until moistened.

2. Transfer to a 9x5-in. loaf pan coated with cooking spray. Bake until a toothpick inserted in center comes out clean, 40-50 minutes. Cool in pan 10 minutes before removing to a wire rack to cool.

1 PIECE: 147 cal., 5g fat (1g sat. fat), 12mg chol., 160mg sod., 21g carb. (3g sugars, 1g fiber), 3g pro.

DIABETIC EXCHANGES: 1½ starch, 1 fat.

HERBED HARVEST VEGETABLE CASSEROLE

I belong to a cooking club, so I try a lot of new recipes. This one has become one of my favorites. I hope your family enjoys it as much as mine does!

—Netty Dyck, St. Catharines, ON

PREP: 15 MIN. • **BAKE:** 1 HOUR 40 MIN. + STANDING • **MAKES:** 8 SERVINGS

- **4 new potatoes, cut in ¼-in. slices**
- **¼ cup butter**
- **1 Tbsp. finely chopped fresh sage or 1 tsp. dried sage**
- **1 Tbsp. finely chopped fresh tarragon or 1 tsp. dried tarragon**
- **3 sweet red bell peppers, seeded and diced**
- **1 onion, thinly sliced**
- **½ cup uncooked long-grain rice**
- **3 medium zucchini, thinly sliced**
- **4 medium tomatoes, sliced**
- **1 cup shredded Swiss cheese**

1. Grease a 2½-qt. baking dish and arrange half the potato slices in overlapping rows. Dot with half the butter. Sprinkle with half the sage, tarragon, peppers, onion, rice and zucchini. Dot with remaining butter and repeat layering.

2. Cover and bake at 350° for 1½ hours or until potatoes are tender. Uncover; top with tomato slices and cheese. Bake 10 minutes longer or until tomatoes are warm and cheese is melted. Remove from oven; cover and let stand for 10 minutes before serving.

1 SERVING: 206 cal., 10g fat (6g sat. fat), 28mg chol., 105mg sod., 24g carb. (6g sugars, 4g fiber), 7g pro.

EASY BATTER ROLLS

The first thing my guests ask when they come for dinner is if I'm serving these dinner rolls. The buns are so light, airy and delicious that I'm constantly asked for the recipe.

—Thomasina Brunner, Gloversville, NY

PREP: 30 MIN. + RISING • **BAKE:** 15 MIN. • **MAKES:** 1 DOZEN

- **3 cups all-purpose flour**
- **2 Tbsp. sugar**
- **1 pkg. (¼ oz.) active dry yeast**
- **1 tsp. salt**
- **1 cup water**
- **2 Tbsp. butter**
- **1 large egg, room temperature**
- **Melted butter**

1. In a large bowl, combine 2 cups flour, sugar, yeast and salt. In a saucepan, heat water and butter to 120°-130°. Add to dry ingredients; beat until blended. Add egg; beat on low speed for 30 seconds, then on high for 3 minutes. Stir in enough of the remaining flour to form a stiff dough. Do not knead. Cover and let rise in a warm place until doubled, about 30 minutes.

2. Stir dough down. Fill 12 greased muffin cups half full. Cover and let rise until doubled, about 15 minutes.

3. Bake at 350° until golden brown, 15-20 minutes. Cool for 1 minute before removing from pan to a wire rack. Brush tops with melted butter.

FREEZE OPTION: Freeze cooled rolls in airtight containers. To use, microwave each roll on high until warmed, 30-45 seconds.

1 ROLL: 147 cal., 3g fat (1g sat. fat), 21mg chol., 219mg sod., 26g carb. (2g sugars, 1g fiber), 4g pro.

GLAZED BABY CARROTS

For a zippy side dish, try this recipe. These brown sugar-glazed carrots come together in no time at all.

—Anita Foster, Fairmount, GA

TAKES: 15 MIN. • **MAKES:** 4 SERVINGS

- **1 lb. fresh, frozen or canned whole baby carrots**
- **Water**
- **2 Tbsp. butter**
- **¼ cup brown sugar**

Cook carrots in a small amount of water until tender. Drain. In a saucepan, combine butter and brown sugar; heat until sugar dissolves. Add carrots and toss to coat. Heat through.

¾ CUP: 142 cal., 6g fat (4g sat. fat), 15mg chol., 152mg sod., 23g carb. (19g sugars, 2g fiber), 1g pro.

KITCHEN TIP: Dark brown sugar contains more molasses than light or golden brown sugar. The two types are generally interchangeable in recipes. If you prefer a bolder flavor, choose dark brown sugar.

CHIVE SMASHED POTATOES

No need to peel the potatoes—in fact, this is the only way we make mashed potatoes anymore. Mixing in the flavored cream cheese is a delightful twist.

—Beverly Norris, Evanston, WY

TAKES: 30 MIN. • **MAKES:** 12 SERVINGS

- **4 lbs. red potatoes, quartered**
- **2 tsp. chicken bouillon granules**
- **1 carton (8 oz.) spreadable chive and onion cream cheese**
- **½ cup half-and-half cream**
- **¼ cup butter, cubed**
- **1 tsp. salt**
- **¼ tsp. pepper**
- **Chopped chives, optional**

1. Place potatoes and bouillon in a Dutch oven and cover with 8 cups water. Bring to a boil. Reduce heat; cover and cook until tender, 15-20 minutes.

2. Drain and return to pan. Mash potatoes with cream cheese, cream, butter, salt and pepper. Garnish with chives.

⅔ CUP: 219 cal., 11g fat (7g sat. fat), 31mg chol., 428mg sod., 26g carb. (3g sugars, 3g fiber), 5g pro.

Beverly's Chive
Smashed
Potatoes

EMILY'S HONEY LIME COLESLAW

Here's a refreshing take on slaw with a honey-lime vinaigrette rather than the traditional mayo. It's a great take-along for all those summer picnics.

—Emily Tyra, Lake Ann, MI

PREP: 20 MIN. + CHILLING • **MAKES:** 8 SERVINGS

- **1½ tsp. grated lime zest**
- **¼ cup lime juice**
- **2 Tbsp. honey**
- **1 garlic clove, minced**
- **½ tsp. salt**
- **¼ tsp. pepper**
- **¼ tsp. crushed red pepper flakes**
- **3 Tbsp. canola oil**
- **1 small head red cabbage (about ¾ lb.), shredded**
- **1 cup shredded carrots (about 2 medium carrots)**
- **2 green onions, thinly sliced**
- **½ cup fresh cilantro leaves**

Whisk together the first 7 ingredients until smooth. Gradually whisk in oil until blended. Combine cabbage, carrots and green onions; toss with lime mixture to lightly coat. Refrigerate, covered, 2 hours. Sprinkle with cilantro.

½ CUP: 86 cal., 5g fat (0 sat. fat), 0 chol., 170mg sod., 10g carb. (7g sugars, 2g fiber), 1g pro.

DIABETIC EXCHANGES: 1 vegetable, 1 fat.

SPINACH & TORTELLINI SOUP

A simple tomato-enhanced broth is perfect for cheese tortellini and fresh spinach. Increase the garlic and add Italian seasoning to suit your taste.

—Debbie Wilson, Burlington, NC

TAKES: 20 MIN. • **MAKES:** 6 SERVINGS (2 QT.)

1 tsp. olive oil
2 garlic cloves, minced
1 can (14½ oz.) no-salt-added diced tomatoes, undrained
3 cans (14½ oz. each) vegetable broth
2 tsp. Italian seasoning
1 pkg. (9 oz.) refrigerated cheese tortellini
4 cups fresh baby spinach
Shredded Parmesan cheese
Freshly ground pepper

1. In a large saucepan, heat oil over medium heat. Add garlic; cook and stir 1 minute. Stir in tomatoes, broth and Italian seasoning; bring to a boil. Add tortellini; bring to a gentle boil. Cook, uncovered, just until tortellini are tender, 7-9 minutes.

2. Stir in spinach. Sprinkle servings with cheese and pepper.

1⅓ CUPS: 164 cal., 5g fat (2g sat. fat), 18mg chol., 799mg sod., 25g carb. (4g sugars, 2g fiber), 7g pro.

SWEET POTATO CRESCENTS

These light-as-air crescent rolls make a delightful accompaniment to any menu. I often serve them as part of our Thanksgiving dinner.

—Rebecca Bailey, Fairbury, NE

PREP: 30 MIN. + RISING • **BAKE:** 15 MIN. • **MAKES:** 3 DOZEN

- **2 pkg. (¼ oz. each) active dry yeast**
- **1 cup warm water (110° to 115°)**
- **1 can (15¾ oz.) cut sweet potatoes, drained and mashed**
- **½ cup sugar**
- **½ cup shortening**
- **1 large egg, room temperature**
- **1½ tsp. salt**
- **5 to 5½ cups all-purpose flour**
- **¼ cup butter, melted**

1. In a large bowl, dissolve yeast in water; let stand for 5 minutes. Beat in the sweet potatoes, sugar, shortening, egg, salt and 3 cups flour. Add enough of the remaining flour to form a stiff dough.

2. Turn onto a floured surface; knead until smooth and elastic, 6-8 minutes. Place in a greased bowl, turning once to grease top. Cover and let rise in a warm place until doubled, about 1 hour.

3. Punch dough down; divide into thirds. Roll each portion into a 12-in. circle; cut each into 12 wedges. Brush with butter. Roll up from the wide end and place, pointed end down, 2 in. apart on greased baking sheets. Cover and let rise until doubled, about 40 minutes.

4. Bake at 375° for 13-15 minutes or until golden brown. Remove from pans to wire racks.

1 ROLL: 123 cal., 4g fat (2g sat. fat), 9mg chol., 119mg sod., 19g carb. (5g sugars, 1g fiber), 2g pro.

ZUCCHINI IN DILL CREAM SAUCE

My husband and I were dairy farmers until we retired in 1967, so I always use fresh, real dairy products in my recipes. This creamy sauce combines all of our favorite foods!

—Josephine Vanden Heuvel, Hart, MI

TAKES: 30 MIN. • **MAKES:** 8 SERVINGS

- **7 cups sliced zucchini (¼-in. slices)**
- **¼ cup finely chopped onion**
- **½ cup water**
- **1 tsp. salt**
- **1 tsp. chicken bouillon granules or 1 chicken bouillon cube**
- **½ tsp. dill weed**
- **2 Tbsp. butter, melted**
- **2 tsp. sugar**
- **1 tsp. lemon juice**
- **2 Tbsp. all-purpose flour**
- **¼ cup sour cream**

SERVE WITH:
No-Fuss Fish Packets, Page 115

1. In a Dutch oven, combine zucchini, onion, water, salt, bouillon and dill; bring to a boil. Add the butter, sugar and lemon juice; mix. Remove from heat; do not drain.

2. Combine flour and sour cream; stir half the mixture into hot zucchini. Return to heat; add remaining cream mixture and cook until thickened.

¾ CUP: 73 cal., 4g fat, 11mg chol., 419mg sod., 8g carb., 2g pro.

DIABETIC EXCHANGES: 1 vegetable, 1 fat.

TEXAS PECAN RICE

For a special side dish, I dressed up an old recipe to give it a little more Texas character. Everyone loved the savory flavor and crunchy pecans.

—Joan Hallford, North Richland Hills, TX

PREP: 30 MIN. • **BAKE:** 1 HOUR • **MAKES:** 10 SERVINGS

- **½ cup unsalted butter, cubed**
- **1½ cups sliced fresh mushrooms**
- **3 green onions, sliced**
- **2 cups uncooked long grain brown rice**
- **1 garlic clove, minced**
- **1½ cups chopped pecans, toasted**
- **½ tsp. salt**
- **½ tsp. dried thyme**
- **½ tsp. pepper**
- **¼ tsp. ground cumin**
- **3 cans (10½ oz. each) condensed beef consomme, undiluted**
- **2¼ cups water**
- **5 bacon strips, cooked and crumbled**
- **Toasted pecan halves, optional**

1. Preheat oven to 400°. In a Dutch oven, heat butter over medium-high heat. Add mushrooms and green onions; cook and stir until tender, 3-5 minutes. Add rice and garlic; cook and stir 3 minutes. Stir in pecans, salt, thyme, pepper and cumin. Add consomme and water; bring to a boil.

2. Bake, covered, until liquid is absorbed and rice is tender, 1-1¼ hours. Transfer to a serving bowl. Top with bacon and, if desired, pecan halves.

¾ CUP: 372 cal., 24g fat (8g sat. fat), 29mg chol., 783mg sod., 32g carb. (2g sugars, 4g fiber), 10g pro.

RED, WHITE & BLUE SUMMER SALAD

Caprese and fresh fruit always remind me of summer. In this salad, I combine the traditional Caprese flavors with summer blueberries and peaches. I also add prosciutto for saltiness, creating a balanced, flavor-packed side dish.

—Emily Falke, Santa Barbara, CA

TAKES: 25 MIN. • **MAKES:** 12 SERVINGS

- **⅔ cup extra virgin olive oil**
- **½ cup julienned fresh basil**
- **⅓ cup white balsamic vinegar**
- **¼ cup julienned fresh mint leaves**
- **2 garlic cloves, minced**
- **2 tsp. Dijon mustard**
- **1 tsp. sea salt**
- **1 tsp. sugar**
- **1 tsp. pepper**
- **2 cups cherry tomatoes**
- **8 cups fresh arugula**
- **1 carton (8 oz.) fresh mozzarella cheese pearls, drained**
- **2 medium peaches, sliced**
- **2 cups fresh blueberries**
- **6 oz. thinly sliced prosciutto, julienned**
- **Additional mint leaves**

1. In a small bowl, whisk the first 9 ingredients. Add tomatoes; let stand while preparing salad.

2. In a large bowl, combine arugula, mozzarella, peach slices, blueberries and prosciutto. Pour tomato mixture over top; toss to coat. Garnish with additional mint leaves. Serve immediately.

1 CUP: 233 cal., 18g fat (5g sat. fat), 27mg chol., 486mg sod., 10g carb. (8g sugars, 2g fiber), 8g pro.

KITCHEN TIP: White balsamic vinegar keeps the colors bright in this sweet-salty salad.

BAKED BEANS MOLE

My son and husband love this hearty side dish that is quick and easy to prepare but yet so flavorful. Chocolate, chili and honey mingle to create a rich, savory flavor that's not too spicy and not too sweet.

—Roxanne Chan, Albany, CA

PREP: 25 MIN. • **BAKE:** 40 MINUTES • **MAKES:** 8 SERVINGS

- **¼ lb. fresh chorizo, crumbled**
- **½ cup chopped onion**
- **½ cup chopped sweet red pepper**
- **1 large garlic clove, minced**
- **1 can (15 oz.) black beans, rinsed and drained**
- **1 can (15 oz.) pinto beans, rinsed and drained**
- **1 can (15 oz.) black-eyed peas, rinsed and drained**
- **1 cup salsa (medium or hot)**
- **1 cup chili sauce**
- **2 Tbsp. honey**
- **1 Tbsp. instant coffee granules**
- **½ tsp. ground cinnamon**
- **2 oz. chopped bittersweet or semisweet chocolate**
- **Minced fresh cilantro**

Preheat oven to 375°. In a large, ovenproof skillet with a lid, cook chorizo, onion, red pepper and garlic over medium heat until sausage is browned, 4-6 minutes. Add next 9 ingredients; mix well. Bake, covered, until mixture is thickened and flavors are blended, about 40 minutes. Sprinkle with cilantro.

⅔ CUP: 284 cal., 7g fat (3g sat. fat), 13mg chol., 989mg sod., 40g carb. (14g sugars, 6g fiber), 11g pro.

KITCHEN TIP: Although this dish is great with several different types of beans, it's equally good with just one.

BABY KALE SALAD WITH AVOCADO-LIME DRESSING

We pull a bunch of ingredients from our garden when we make this salad of greens, zucchini and sweet onion. The yogurt dressing layers on big lime flavor.
—Suzanna Esther, State College, PA

TAKES: 20 MIN. • **MAKES:** 4 SERVINGS (3/4 CUP DRESSING)

- **6 cups baby kale salad blend**
- **1 cup julienned zucchini**
- **1/2 cup thinly sliced sweet onion**
- **1/2 cup fat-free plain yogurt**
- **2 Tbsp. lime juice**
- **1 garlic clove, minced**
- **1/4 tsp. salt**
- **1/8 tsp. pepper**
- **1/2 medium ripe avocado, peeled**
- **3 green onions, chopped**
- **2 Tbsp. minced fresh parsley**

In a large bowl, combine salad blend, zucchini and sweet onion. Place remaining ingredients in blender; cover and process until smooth. Divide the salad mixture among 4 plates; drizzle with the dressing.

1 1/2 CUPS SALAD WITH 3 TBSP. DRESSING: 74 cal., 3g fat (1g sat. fat), 1mg chol., 197mg sod., 10g carb. (4g sugars, 4g fiber), 4g pro.

DIABETIC EXCHANGES: 2 vegetable, 1/2 fat.

PARMESAN GARLIC BREADSTICKS

These tender breadsticks fill the kitchen with a tempting aroma when they are baking, and they're wonderful served warm. My family tells me I can't make them enough.

—Gaylene Anderson, Sandy, UT

PREP: 40 MIN. + RISING • **BAKE:** 10 MIN. • **MAKES:** 3 DOZEN

- **2 pkg. (¼ oz. each) active dry yeast**
- **1½ cups warm water (110° to 115°)**
- **½ cup warm 2% milk (110° to 115°)**
- **3 Tbsp. sugar**
- **3 Tbsp. plus ¼ cup butter, softened, divided**
- **1 tsp. salt**
- **4½ to 5½ cups all-purpose flour**
- **¼ cup grated Parmesan cheese**
- **½ tsp. garlic salt**

1. In a large bowl, dissolve yeast in warm water. Add the milk, sugar, 3 Tbsp. butter, salt and 2 cups flour. Beat until smooth. Stir in enough remaining flour to form a soft dough.

2. Turn onto a floured surface; knead until smooth and elastic, 6-8 minutes. Place in a greased bowl, turning once to grease top. Cover and let rise in a warm place until doubled, about 45 minutes.

3. Punch the dough down. Turn onto a floured surface; divide into 36 pieces. Shape each piece into a 6-in. rope. Place 2 in. apart on greased baking sheets. Cover and let rise until doubled, about 25 minutes.

4. Melt remaining butter; brush over dough. Sprinkle with Parmesan cheese and garlic salt. Bake at 400° until golden brown, 8-10 minutes. Remove from pans to wire racks.

1 BREADSTICK: 86 cal., 3g fat (2g sat. fat), 7mg chol., 126mg sod., 13g carb. (1g sugars, 0 fiber), 2g pro.

GARDEN SALAD WITH CHICKPEAS

Discover a new favorite when you jazz up spring green salad mix with garden-fresh greats, a homemade vinaigrette, chickpeas and crumbled goat cheese.

—Taste of Home *Test Kitchen*

TAKES: 25 MIN. • **MAKES:** 6 SERVINGS

- **⅓ cup olive oil**
- **¼ cup lemon juice**
- **2 Tbs. red wine vinegar**
- **½ tsp. salt**
- **¼ tsp. pepper**
- **¼ tsp. garlic powder**

SALAD

- **1 can (15 ounces) garbanzo beans or chickpeas, rinsed and drained**
- **2 medium carrots, julienned**
- **1 medium zucchini, julienned**
- **½ cup chopped tomato**
- **4 green onions, thinly sliced**
- **4 radishes, thinly sliced**
- **½ cup chopped pecans, toasted**
- **½ cup coarsely chopped fresh parsley**
- **½ cup crumbled goat cheese**
- **6 cups spring mix salad greens**

1. In a small bowl, whisk oil, lemon juice, vinegar, salt, pepper and garlic powder.

2. In a large bowl, combine chickpeas, carrots, zucchini, tomato, green onions, radishes, pecans, parsley and cheese. Stir in ½ cup dressing. Arrange greens in a serving bowl; top with chickpea mixture. Drizzle with remaining dressing.

1 SERVING: 294 calories, 23g fat (4g saturated fat), 12mg cholesterol, 394mg sodium, 21g carbohydrate (5g sugars, 7g fiber), 7g protein.

PUMPKIN & CAULIFLOWER GARLIC MASH

I wanted healthy alternatives to my family's favorite recipes. Pumpkin, cauliflower and thyme make an amazing dish. You'll never miss plain mashed potatoes again.

—Kari Wheaton, South Beloit, IL

TAKES: 25 MIN. • MAKES: 6 SERVINGS

- **1 medium head cauliflower, broken into florets (about 6 cups)**
- **3 garlic cloves**
- **⅓ cup spreadable cream cheese**
- **1 can (15 oz.) solid-pack pumpkin**
- **1 Tbsp. minced fresh thyme**
- **1 tsp. salt**
- **¼ tsp. cayenne pepper**
- **¼ tsp. pepper**

1. Place 1 in. of water in a Dutch oven; bring to a boil. Add cauliflower and garlic cloves; cook, covered, until tender, 8-10 minutes. Drain; transfer to a food processor.

2. Add remaining ingredients; process until smooth. Return to pan; heat through, stirring occasionally.

⅔ CUP: 87 cal., 4g fat (2g sat. fat), 9mg chol., 482mg sod., 12g carb. (5g sugars, 4g fiber), 4g pro.

DIABETIC EXCHANGES: 1 vegetable, ½ starch, ½ fat.

MAPLE-GLAZED GREEN BEANS

After I picked my first green beans one year, I wanted to make a savory dish that was unique, quick and packed with flavor. I loved this so much I couldn't stop eating it, so the next day I picked more beans and made this delicious side dish again.

—Merry Graham, Newhall, CA

TAKES: 25 MIN. • **MAKES:** 4 SERVINGS

- **3 cups cut fresh green beans**
- **1 large onion, chopped**
- **4 bacon strips, cut into 1-in. pieces**
- **½ cup dried cranberries**
- **¼ cup maple syrup**
- **¼ tsp. salt**
- **¼ tsp. pepper**
- **1 Tbsp. bourbon, optional**

1. In a large saucepan, place steamer basket over 1 in. of water. Place beans in basket. Bring water to a boil. Reduce heat to maintain a low boil; steam, covered, until crisp-tender, about 4-5 minutes.

2. Meanwhile, in a large skillet, cook onion and bacon over medium heat until bacon is crisp; drain. Stir cranberries, syrup, salt, pepper and, if desired, bourbon into onion mixture. Add beans; heat through, tossing to combine.

¾ CUP: 173 cal., 3g fat (1g sat. fat), 7mg chol., 302mg sod., 35g carb. (24g sugars, 4g fiber), 4g pro.

OLIVE & ONION QUICK BREAD

I've been baking for over 50 years and I never get tired of trying new recipes for my family, friends and co-workers. Baking actually relaxes me. I feel like an artist creating a masterpiece of love. This savory loaf makes a great gift.

—Paula Marchesi, Lenhartsville, PA

PREP: 15 MIN. • **BAKE:** 45 MIN. + COOLING • **MAKES:** 1 LOAF (12 SLICES)

- **1 Tbsp. canola oil**
- **1 medium onion, finely chopped**
- **2 cups all-purpose flour**
- **1 Tbsp. minced fresh rosemary**
- **1 tsp. baking soda**
- **½ tsp. salt**
- **2 large eggs, room temperature**
- **1 cup buttermilk**
- **2 Tbsp. butter, melted**
- **¼ cup plus 2 Tbsp. shredded sharp cheddar cheese, divided**
- **¼ cup each chopped pitted green and ripe olives**

SERVE WITH:
Smoky Macaroni & Cheese, Page 272

1. Preheat oven to 350°. In a skillet, heat oil over medium-high heat. Add onion; cook and stir until tender, 2-3 minutes. Remove from heat.

2. In a large bowl, whisk flour, rosemary, baking soda and salt. In another bowl, whisk eggs, buttermilk and melted butter until blended. Add to flour mixture; stir just until moistened. Fold in ¼ cup cheese, olives and onion.

3. Transfer to a greased 8x4-in. loaf pan. Bake 40 minutes. Sprinkle remaining cheese over top. Bake until a toothpick inserted in center comes out clean, 5-10 minutes longer. Cool in pan 10 minutes before removing to a wire rack to cool.

1 PIECE: 150 cal., 6g fat (2g sat. fat), 41mg chol., 373mg sod., 18g carb. (1g sugars, 1g fiber), 5g pro.

CHAPTER 5

TASTY ODDS & ENDS

Looking to make dinner extra special? Consider surprising your family with savory appetizers, sweet treats and everything in between. Whether you're rounding out a menu or simply need to bring a dish to pass, this enticing chapter has the answer.

HERBED FETA DIP

Guests keep coming back for more of this thick, zesty dip full of Mediterranean flavor. The feta cheese and fresh mint complement each other beautifully, creating the perfect sidekick for crunchy carrots, toasted pita chips, sliced baguettes or any other dipper you fancy.

—Rebecca Ray, Chicago, IL

TAKES: 25 MIN. • **MAKES:** 3 CUPS

- **½ cup packed fresh parsley sprigs**
- **½ cup fresh mint leaves**
- **½ cup olive oil**
- **2 garlic cloves, peeled**
- **½ tsp. pepper**
- **4 cups (16 oz.) crumbled feta cheese**
- **3 Tbsp. lemon juice**
- **Assorted fresh vegetables**

In a food processor, combine the first 5 ingredients; cover and pulse until finely chopped. Add cheese and lemon juice; process until creamy. Serve with vegetables.

¼ CUP: 176 cal., 15g fat (5g sat. fat), 20mg chol., 361mg sod., 2g carb. (0 sugars, 1g fiber), 7g pro.

SPICY POTATOES WITH GARLIC AIOLI

This is my take on Spanish *patatas bravas*. I toss the potatoes in a flavorful spice mix, then bake them to a crispy golden brown. The garlic aioli guarantees a crowd-pleasing appetizer or side every time.

—John Stiver, Bowen Island, BC

PREP: 35 MIN. • **BAKE:** 25 MIN. • **MAKES:** 10 SERVINGS (1¾ CUPS AIOLI)

- **3 lbs. medium Yukon Gold potatoes, cut into 1½-in. cubes (about 8 potatoes)**
- **2 Tbsp. olive oil**
- **2 garlic cloves, minced**
- **2 Tbsp. smoked paprika**
- **2 tsp. garlic powder**
- **1½ tsp. chili powder**
- **1½ tsp. ground cumin**
- **¼ tsp. salt**
- **¼ tsp. crushed red pepper flakes**
- **⅛ tsp. pepper**

AIOLI

- **1½ cups mayonnaise**
- **3 Tbsp. lemon juice**
- **3 garlic cloves, minced**
- **1 Tbsp. minced fresh chives plus additional for topping**
- **1 tsp. red wine vinegar**
- **¼ tsp. salt**
- **¼ tsp. pepper**

1. Preheat oven to 375°. Place potatoes in a Dutch oven; add water to cover. Bring to a boil. Reduce heat; cook, uncovered, 8-10 minutes or until just tender. Drain; pat dry with paper towels. Transfer potatoes to a mixing bowl. Toss potatoes in oil and minced garlic to coat evenly.

2. Combine the smoked paprika, garlic powder, chili powder, cumin, salt, red pepper flakes and pepper; sprinkle over the potatoes. Gently toss to coat. Transfer the potatoes to 2 greased 15x10x1-in. baking pans, spreading into a single layer. Bake until crispy, about 25 minutes, stirring potatoes and rotating pans halfway through cooking.

3. For aioli, combine ingredients until blended. Transfer potatoes to a serving platter; sprinkle with chives. Serve warm with aioli.

¾ CUP POTATOES WITH ABOUT 3 TBSP. AIOLI: 469 cal., 34g fat (5g sat. fat), 3mg chol., 396mg sod., 37g carb. (3g sugars, 4g fiber), 5g pro.

KITCHEN TIP: The seasoning blend gives these potatoes a nice kick; smoked paprika makes them taste as if they were cooked over an open fire. Remember this spice mix the next time you're prepping Tater Tots, and sprinkle some on for an upgrade.

GOODBYE CITY, HELLO COUNTRY!

BY KELLEY BRACKEN, RURAL RETREAT, VIRGINIA

Excitement gripped us as the RV pulled out of our California driveway for the last time. I could hardly believe we were actually doing it.

Though my family lived in the city, we had always loved the idea of moving to the country. As we learned more about where our food came from, our desire to live off the land grew stronger.

Then one day my parents, Philip and Lynda, decided to list our house for sale and see what would happen. Just like that, we sold our home, bought an RV and drove in search of a farm.

After much looking, we finally put down roots in Rural Retreat, Virginia. God blessed us more than we ever imagined, as the gently flowing streams, red barns and lush rolling pastures around us became home. Our friendly neighbors were excited about our farming vision.

To this day we are so grateful for the help and support of these neighbors who have become like family. We named our place My Shepherd's Farm, inspired by the words of Psalm 23, "The Lord is my shepherd; I shall not want."

Dad, who was born and raised in Ireland, was able to relive his childhood memories. While picking cabbage to sell at the farmers market, he told my sister, Michelle, and me stories of how, as a boy, he'd load his wheelbarrow full of homegrown cabbage to sell door to door in the early morning.

During the summers he spent at his uncle's farm, he imagined having a farm of his own one day. He has always been an extremely hard worker, and it is so wonderful to see him living his dream.

Today, most of what we eat we produce on our land. We sell pastured pork, chicken and eggs

Country dad Philip (left) loves living off the land. This life makes Kelley (top right) and her sister, Michelle, jump for joy. Kelley's nieces (above) explore after splashing in a nearby spring.

along with our homemade deodorants, lip balms and soaps. We make our own hay, keep bees, grow vegetable gardens and do our own canning. We are learning how to raise our food sustainably, without hormones, antibiotics or pesticides.

Since moving to the farm, I've learned countless lessons. I know what it's like to have meals where everything on the plate was grown on our farmland, and I understand that these flavors are unlike anything from the store.

I have learned that pigs are stronger than they look, and there is no need for a gym membership after hauling hay. I've tasted honey straight from the hive and watched as hens hatch and raise their chicks with such care.

It's true that you never really get to the bottom of a to-do list when you live on a farm. But I've come to appreciate the blooms of spring so much more after spending winter breaking ice.

I've learned how much electric fence can hurt. I've experienced sleeping in a field with a cow about to calve, and raising friendly cows that respond to their names.

A normally tame sow showed me she can run quite fast after she's had piglets; in the process, Michelle showed me how quickly she can hop a fence. I've watched kids from the city delight in the joys of farm life for the first time.

We've spent whole evenings catching lightning bugs in Mason jars, swinging on the porch swing and gazing at the stars. We have ridden cows and pigs, and we've face-planted in the mud when the overzealous pigs have run to greet us at once.

My family has created so many memories for which we are grateful to God, and we are excited to know we have so much yet to learn.

WHITE ALMOND NO-BAKE COOKIES

My daughter and I like teaming up to create new recipes. One day when we were out of chocolate chips, we grabbed the white chips in the cupboard and hit on a new favorite.

—Debbie Johnson, Winona Lake, IN

PREP: 25 MIN. • **COOK:** 5 MIN. + CHILLING • **MAKES:** ABOUT 3½ DOZEN

2 cups sugar
½ cup butter, cubed
½ cup 2% milk
1 cup white baking chips
½ tsp. almond extract
3 cups old-fashioned oats
1 cup dried cherries or dried cranberries, optional

1. In a large saucepan, combine the sugar, butter and milk. Cook and stir over medium heat until butter is melted and sugar is dissolved. Remove from heat. Stir in baking chips and extract until smooth. Add oats and, if desired, cherries; stir until coated.

2. Drop by rounded tablespoonfuls onto waxed paper-lined baking sheets. Refrigerate until set, about 30 minutes. Store in an airtight container in the refrigerator.

1 COOKIE: 101 cal., 4g fat (2g sat. fat), 7mg chol., 23mg sod., 16g carb. (12g sugars, 1g fiber), 1g pro.

OLD-FASHIONED FRUIT COMPOTE

This warm spiced fruit can simmer while you make the other dishes on your menu. For even easier meal prep, assemble the compote a day ahead and reheat before serving.

—Shirley Glaab, Hattiesburg, MS

PREP: 15 MIN. • **COOK:** 1 HOUR • **MAKES:** 8 CUPS

- **1 can (20 oz.) pineapple chunks, undrained**
- **1 can (15¼ oz.) sliced peaches, undrained**
- **1 can (11 oz.) mandarin oranges, undrained**
- **1 pkg. (18 oz.) pitted dried plums (prunes)**
- **2 pkg. (3½ oz. each) dried blueberries**
- **1 pkg. (6 oz.) dried apricots**
- **½ cup golden raisins**
- **4 lemon zest strips**
- **1 cinnamon stick (3 in.)**
- **1 jar (10 oz.) maraschino cherries, drained**

SERVE WITH:
Cider-Glazed Ham,
Page 183

Drain pineapple, peaches and oranges, reserving the juices; set the drained fruit aside. In a Dutch oven, combine the fruit juice, dried fruits, lemon zest strips and cinnamon stick. Bring to a boil. Reduce heat; cover and simmer until the dried fruit is tender, about 30 minutes. Add reserved canned fruit and maraschino cherries; heat just until warmed through. Serve warm or at room temperature.

¼ CUP: 126 cal., 0 fat (0 sat. fat), 0 chol., 4mg sod., 31g carb. (22g sugars, 2g fiber), 1g pro.

SMOKY MACARONI & CHEESE

After discovering this recipe years ago in a magazine, I kept tweaking the ingredients until I hit on the perfect combination. You can make this in the oven, but we think grilling or smoking is the way to go.

—Stacey Dull, Gettysburg, OH

PREP: 40 MIN. • **GRILL:** 20 MIN. + STANDING • **MAKES:** 2 CASSEROLES (8 SERVINGS EACH)

- **6 cups small pasta shells**
- **12 oz. Velveeta, cut into small cubes**
- **2 cups shredded smoked cheddar cheese, divided**
- **1 cup shredded cheddar cheese**
- **1 cup 2% milk**
- **4 large eggs, lightly beaten**
- **¾ cup heavy whipping cream**
- **⅔ cup half-and-half cream**
- **½ cup shredded provolone cheese**
- **½ cup shredded Colby-Monterey Jack cheese**
- **½ cup shredded pepper jack cheese**
- **1 tsp. salt**
- **½ tsp. pepper**
- **½ tsp. smoked paprika**
- **½ tsp. liquid smoke, optional**
- **Dash cayenne pepper, optional**
- **8 bacon strips, cooked and crumbled, optional**

1. Preheat grill or smoker to 350°. Cook the pasta according to package directions for al dente. Drain and transfer to a large bowl. Stir in Velveeta, 1 cup smoked cheddar, cheddar cheese, milk, eggs, heavy whipping cream, half-and-half, provolone, Colby-Monterey Jack, pepper jack, salt, pepper, paprika and, if desired, liquid smoke and cayenne pepper.

2. Transfer to 2 greased 13x9-in. baking pans; sprinkle with remaining 1 cup smoked cheddar cheese. Place on the grill or smoker rack. Grill or smoke, covered, until a thermometer reads at least 160°, 20-25 minutes, rotating the pans partway through cooking. Do not overcook. Let stand 10 minutes before serving; if desired, sprinkle with bacon.

1 CUP: 403 cal., 23g fat (13g sat. fat), 117mg chol., 670mg sod., 30g carb. (4g sugars, 1g fiber), 18g pro.

HOMEMADE CHURROS

Does your family love churros? You may be surprised how easy it is to make a batch of those fried cinnamon-sugar goodies in your own kitchen.

—Taste of Home *Test Kitchen*

PREP: 15 MIN. + COOLING • **COOK:** 20 MIN. • **MAKES:** ABOUT 1 DOZEN

½ cup water
½ cup 2% milk
1 Tbsp. canola oil
¼ tsp. salt
1 cup all-purpose flour
1 large egg, room temperature
¼ tsp. grated lemon zest
Additional oil for frying
½ cup sugar
¼ tsp. ground cinnamon

1. In a large saucepan, bring the water, milk, oil and salt to a boil. Add flour all at once and stir until a smooth ball forms. Transfer to a large bowl; let stand for 5 minutes.

2. Beat on medium-high speed for 1 minute or until the dough softens. Add the egg and lemon zest; beat for 1-2 minutes. Set aside to cool.

3. In a deep cast-iron or heavy skillet, heat 1 in. oil to 375°. Insert a large star tip in a pastry bag; fill with the dough. On a baking sheet, pipe dough into 4-in. strips.

4. Transfer strips to skillet and fry until golden brown on both sides. Drain on paper towels. Combine the sugar and cinnamon; sprinkle over churros. Serve warm.

1 CHURRO: 122 cal., 5g fat (1g sat. fat), 17mg chol., 60mg sod., 17g carb. (9g sugars, 0 fiber), 2g pro.

CREAMY CARAMEL MOCHA

Indulge in a coffeehouse-style beverage at Christmastime or any time at all. With whipped cream and a butterscotch drizzle, this mocha treat will perk up even the sleepiest person at the table.

—Taste of Home *Test Kitchen*

TAKES: 20 MIN. • **MAKES:** 6 SERVINGS

- **½ cup heavy whipping cream**
- **1 Tbsp. confectioners' sugar**
- **1 tsp. vanilla extract, divided**
- **¼ cup Dutch-processed cocoa**
- **1½ cups half-and-half cream**
- **4 cups hot strong brewed coffee**
- **½ cup caramel flavoring syrup**
- **Butterscotch-caramel ice cream topping**

1. In a small bowl, beat whipping cream until it begins to thicken. Add the confectioners' sugar and ½ tsp. vanilla; beat until stiff peaks form.

2. In a large saucepan over medium heat, whisk cocoa and half-and-half cream until smooth. Heat until bubbles form around the sides of pan. Whisk in coffee, caramel syrup and remaining vanilla. Top servings with whipped cream; drizzle with butterscotch topping.

SLOW-COOKER CREAMY CARAMEL MOCHA: Prepare the whipped cream as directed. Whisk together the cocoa, half-and-half cream, coffee, caramel syrup and remaining vanilla in a 3-qt. slow cooker. Cook, covered, 2-3 hours or until heated through. Serve as directed.

1 CUP COFFEE WITH 2 TBSP. WHIPPED CREAM: 220 cal., 14g fat (9g sat. fat), 57mg chol., 38mg sod., 19g carb. (16g sugars, 1g fiber), 3g pro.

CHIP-CRUSTED GRILLED CORN

For my version of Mexican street corn, I roll the ears in crushed tortilla chips. Have fun trying different chip flavors, such as ranch dressing or jalapeno.

—Crystal Schlueter, Northglenn, CO

TAKES: 30 MIN. • **MAKES:** 6 SERVINGS

- **¾ cup mayonnaise**
- **¼ cup sour cream**
- **2 Tbsp. minced fresh cilantro**
- **½ tsp. salt**
- **¼ tsp. cayenne pepper**
- **¼ tsp. pepper**
- **1 cup crushed tortilla chips**
- **6 medium ears sweet corn, husks removed**
- **Lime wedges**

1. In a small bowl, combine the first 6 ingredients. Refrigerate, covered, until serving. Place the tortilla chips in a shallow bowl. Grill corn, covered, over medium heat 15-20 minutes or until tender, turning occasionally.

2. When cool enough to handle, spread corn with mayonnaise mixture; roll in chips. Grill corn, covered, 1-2 minutes longer or until lightly browned. Serve with lime wedges.

1 EAR OF CORN: 355 cal., 27g fat (5g sat. fat), 17mg chol., 405mg sod., 26g carb. (7g sugars, 2g fiber), 4g pro.

KITCHEN TIP: Turn ears of corn into an easy-to-eat veggie bowl with just a few easy steps. Simply cut the grilled corn off the cob and toss the corn with the mayonnaise mixture. Top it all off with the crushed chips and lime wedges.

CINNAMON CHIP CHAI-SPICED SNICKERDOODLES

Here's a yummy way to use one of my favorite ingredients—cinnamon chips. I stock up on them during the holiday season so I have plenty to last during the year.

—Marietta Slater, Justin, TX

PREP: 30 MIN. + CHILLING • **BAKE:** 15 MIN./BATCH + COOLING • **MAKES:** ABOUT 6 DOZEN

½ cup sugar
2 tsp. ground cardamom
2 tsp. ground cinnamon
½ tsp. ground ginger
½ tsp. ground cloves
¼ tsp. ground nutmeg

DOUGH

½ cup butter, softened
½ cup shortening
1 cup sugar
2 large eggs, room temperature
1 tsp. vanilla extract
2¾ cups all-purpose flour
2 tsp. cream of tartar
1 tsp. baking soda
Dash salt
1 pkg. (10 oz.) cinnamon baking chips

1. Preheat oven to 350°. For the spiced sugar, mix the first 6 ingredients.

2. In a large bowl, cream the butter, shortening, sugar and 2 Tbsp. spiced sugar until light and fluffy, 5-7 minutes. Beat in eggs and vanilla. In another bowl, whisk together flour, cream of tartar, baking soda and salt; gradually beat into creamed mixture. Stir in baking chips. Refrigerate, covered, until firm enough to shape, about 1 hour.

3. Shape dough into 1-in. balls; roll in remaining spiced sugar. Place 2 in. apart on greased baking sheets.

4. Bake until set, 11-13 minutes. Remove from pans to wire racks to cool.

1 COOKIE: 81 cal., 4g fat (2g sat. fat), 9mg chol., 59mg sod., 10g carb. (7g sugars, 0 fiber), 1g pro.

TOMATO CHEESE BREAD

My husband and our two children are mostly meat-and-potato eaters. They always make an exception for this bread! We milk 180 cows and have a large garden, so I love to cook with dairy and fresh veggies. When I tried this recipe, it was an instant favorite. It also makes a great appetizer for parties.

—Penney Kester, Springville, NY

PREP: 20 MIN. • **BAKE:** 25 MIN. + STANDING • **MAKES:** 12 SERVINGS

- **2 Tbsp. butter**
- **1 medium onion, minced**
- **1 cup shredded cheddar cheese**
- **½ cup sour cream**
- **¼ cup mayonnaise**
- **¾ tsp. salt**
- **¼ tsp. pepper**
- **¼ tsp. dried oregano**
- **Pinch rubbed sage**
- **2 cups biscuit/baking mix**
- **⅔ cup 2% milk**
- **3 medium tomatoes, cut into ¼-in. slices**
- **Paprika**

1. Preheat oven to 400°. In a small skillet, heat butter over medium heat. Add the onion and cook until tender. Remove from heat. Stir in the cheese, sour cream, mayonnaise and seasonings; set aside.

2. In a bowl, combine the baking mix and milk to form a soft dough. Turn dough onto a well-floured surface; knead lightly 10-12 times. Pat into a greased 13x9-in. baking dish, pushing dough up sides of dish to form a shallow rim. Arrange tomato slices over the top. Spread with topping; sprinkle with paprika.

3. Bake for 25 minutes. Let stand for 10 minutes before cutting.

1 PIECE: 209 cal., 14g fat (6g sat. fat), 26mg chol., 521mg sod., 17g carb. (3g sugars, 1g fiber), 5g pro.

BUTTERSCOTCH-RUM RAISIN TREATS

I love making rum raisin rice pudding for the holidays, and that traditional dessert inspired this confection. Crispy rice cereal adds crunch, but toasted coconut, nuts or candied pineapple could do the job, too.

—Crystal Schlueter, Northglenn, CO

TAKES: 20 MIN. • **MAKES:** ABOUT 4½ DOZEN

- **1 pkg. (10 to 11 oz.) butterscotch chips**
- **1 pkg. (10 to 12 oz.) white baking chips**
- **½ tsp. rum extract**
- **3 cups Rice Krispies**
- **1 cup raisins**

1. Line 56 mini-muffin cups with paper liners. In a large bowl, combine butterscotch and white chips. Microwave, uncovered, on high for 30 seconds; stir. Microwave in additional 30-second intervals, stirring until smooth.

2. Stir in extract, Rice Krispies and raisins. Drop by rounded tablespoonfuls into prepared mini-muffin cups. Chill until set.

FREEZE OPTION: Freeze treats in freezer containers, separating layers with waxed paper. Thaw before serving.

1 TREAT: 76 cal., 4g fat (3g sat. fat), 1mg chol., 21mg sod., 11g carb. (9g sugars, 0 fiber), 0 pro.

SOFT BEER PRETZEL NUGGETS

What goes together better than beer and pretzels? These from-scratch nuggets make a great snack or side for sandwiches and burgers.

—Alyssa Wilhite, Whitehouse, TX

PREP: 1 HOUR + RISING • **BAKE:** 10 MIN./BATCH • **MAKES:** 8 DOZEN

- **1 bottle (12 oz.) amber beer or nonalcoholic beer**
- **1 pkg. (1/4 oz.) active dry yeast**
- **2 Tbsp. unsalted butter, melted**
- **2 Tbsp. sugar**
- **1 1/2 tsp. salt**
- **4 to 4 1/2 cups all-purpose flour**
- **10 cups water**
- **2/3 cup baking soda**

TOPPING

- **1 large egg yolk**
- **1 Tbsp. water**
- **Coarse salt, optional**

1. In a small saucepan, heat the beer to 110°-115°; remove from heat. Stir in the yeast until dissolved. In a large bowl, combine the butter, sugar, salt, yeast mixture and 3 cups flour; beat on medium speed until smooth. Stir in enough remaining flour to form a soft dough (dough will be sticky).

2. Turn dough onto a floured surface; knead until smooth and elastic, 6-8 minutes. Place in a greased bowl, turning once to grease the top. Cover and let rise in a warm place until doubled, about 1 hour.

3. Preheat oven to 425°. Punch dough down. Turn onto a lightly floured surface; divide and shape into 8 balls. Roll each into a 12-in. rope. Cut each rope into 1-in. pieces.

4. In a Dutch oven, bring 10 cups water and baking soda to a boil. Drop the pretzel nuggets, 12 at a time, into boiling water. Cook for 30 seconds. Remove with a slotted spoon; drain well on paper towels.

5. Place on greased baking sheets. In a small bowl, whisk the egg yolk and 1 Tbsp. water; brush over the pretzels. Sprinkle with coarse salt if desired. Bake 10-12 minutes or until golden brown. Remove from pans to a wire rack to cool.

FREEZE OPTION: Freeze the cooled pretzel nuggets in airtight containers. To use, thaw at room temperature or, if desired, microwave on high 20-30 seconds or until heated through.

6 PRETZEL NUGGETS: 144 cal., 2g fat (1g sat. fat), 8mg chol., 302mg sod., 26g carb. (2g sugars, 1g fiber), 4g pro.

KITCHEN TIP: Use the same dough to make pretzel rolls. Simply divide and shape the dough into 8 balls; roll each into a 14-in. rope. Starting at 1 end of each rope, loosely wrap the dough around itself to form a coil. Boil, top and bake as directed.

FESTIVE CRANBERRY DRINK

Warm or cold? Take your pick! This spiced cranberry beverage is delightful either way. The pretty color draws you in, and the sweet-tart flavor seals the deal.

—Dixie Terry, Goreville, IL

PREP: 25 MIN. • **COOK:** 20 MIN. • **MAKES:** 3 QT.

- **4 cups fresh or frozen cranberries**
- **3 qt. water, divided**
- **1¾ cups sugar**
- **1 cup orange juice**
- **⅔ cup lemon juice**
- **½ cup Red Hots**
- **12 whole cloves**

1. In a Dutch oven, combine the cranberries and 1 qt. water. Cook over medium heat until berries pop, about 15 minutes. Remove from the heat. Strain through a fine strainer, pressing mixture with a spoon; discard skins. Return cranberry pulp and juice to the pan.

2. Stir in the sugar, juices, Red Hots and remaining water. Place cloves on a double thickness of cheesecloth. Bring up corners of cloth and tie with kitchen string to form a bag; add to juice mixture. Bring to a boil; cook and stir until sugar and Red Hots are dissolved.

3. Remove from the heat. Strain through a fine mesh sieve or cheesecloth. Discard spice bag. Serve drink warm or cold.

1 CUP: 178 cal., 0 fat (0 sat. fat), 0 chol., 1mg sod., 46g carb. (39g sugars, 2g fiber), 0 pro.

LEMON GELATO

While vacationing in Italy, I fell in love with gelato. My favorite was lemon because Italian lemons have an intense flavor. This recipe brings back wonderful memories of our trip.

—Gail Wang, Troy, MI

PREP: 30 MIN. • **PROCESS:** 20 MIN. + FREEZING • **MAKES:** 1½ QT.

- **1 cup whole milk**
- **1 cup sugar**
- **5 large egg yolks, lightly beaten**
- **3 Tbsp. grated lemon zest**
- **¾ cup fresh lemon juice (about 5 lemons)**
- **2 cups heavy whipping cream**

1. In a small heavy saucepan, heat milk to 175°; stir in sugar until dissolved. Whisk a small amount of hot mixture into egg yolks. Return all to the pan, whisking constantly. Add lemon zest. Cook over low heat until the mixture is just thick enough to coat a metal spoon and a thermometer reads at least 160°, stirring constantly. Do not allow to boil.

2. Remove immediately from the heat; stir in lemon juice and cream. Place in a bowl. Press plastic wrap onto the surface of custard; refrigerate several hours or overnight.

3. Fill the cylinder of ice cream freezer two-thirds full; freeze according to manufacturer's directions. (Refrigerate remaining mixture until ready to freeze.) Transfer the ice cream to freezer containers, allowing headspace for expansion. Freeze 2-4 hours or until firm. Repeat with remaining mixture.

⅔ CUP: 361 cal., 26g fat (15g sat. fat), 213mg chol., 40mg sod., 31g carb. (27g sugars, 0 fiber), 4g pro.

SWEET ONION PIMIENTO CHEESE DEVILED EGGS

For my mother's 92nd birthday celebration, we had pimiento-topped deviled eggs as part of the spread. They're timeless and always in good taste.

—Linda Foreman, Locust Grove, OK

TAKES: 15 MIN. • **MAKES:** 1 DOZEN

- **6 hard-boiled large eggs**
- **¼ cup finely shredded sharp cheddar cheese**
- **2 Tbsp. mayonnaise**
- **4 tsp. diced pimientos, drained**
- **2 tsp. finely chopped sweet onion**
- **1 tsp. Dijon mustard**
- **1 small garlic clove, minced**
- **¼ tsp. salt**
- **⅛ tsp. pepper**
- **Additional diced pimientos and finely shredded sharp cheddar cheese**

Cut eggs lengthwise in half. Remove yolks, reserving whites. In a bowl, mash yolks. Stir in cheese, mayonnaise, pimientos, onion, mustard, garlic, salt and pepper. Spoon or pipe mixture into egg whites. Sprinkle with additional pimientos and cheese. Refrigerate, covered, until serving.

1 STUFFED EGG HALF: 67 cal., 5g fat (2g sat. fat), 96mg chol., 128mg sod., 1g carb. (0 sugars, 0 fiber), 4g pro.

CHAPTER 6

MEMORY-MAKING DESSERTS

Few things top off family dinners like a lip-smacking sweet. From cakes layered with flavor to pies bursting with berry goodness, homemade desserts steal the show at Sunday dinners, holiday parties and casual get-togethers alike. Turn here for the impressive specialties that will earn you a blue ribbon from family and friends.

SANDY'S CHOCOLATE CAKE

Years ago, I drove 4½ hours to a cake contest, holding my entry on my lap the whole way. But it paid off. One bite and you'll see why this velvety beauty was named the best chocolate cake and won first prize.

—Sandy Johnson, Tioga, PA

PREP: 30 MIN. • **BAKE:** 30 MIN. + COOLING • **MAKES:** 16 SERVINGS

- **1 cup butter, softened**
- **3 cups packed brown sugar**
- **4 large eggs, room temperature**
- **2 tsp. vanilla extract**
- **2⅔ cups all-purpose flour**
- **¾ cup baking cocoa**
- **3 tsp. baking soda**
- **½ tsp. salt**
- **1⅓ cups sour cream**
- **1⅓ cups boiling water**

FROSTING

- **½ cup butter, cubed**
- **3 oz. unsweetened chocolate, chopped**
- **3 oz. semisweet chocolate, chopped**
- **5 cups confectioners' sugar**
- **1 cup sour cream**
- **2 tsp. vanilla extract**

1. Preheat oven to 350°. Grease and flour three 9-in. round baking pans.

2. In a large bowl, cream butter and brown sugar until light and fluffy, 5-7 minutes. Add eggs, 1 at a time, beating well after each addition. Beat in the vanilla. In another bowl, whisk flour, cocoa, baking soda and salt; add to creamed mixture alternately with sour cream, beating well after each addition. Stir in the boiling water until blended.

3. Transfer to prepared pans. Bake until a toothpick comes out clean, 30-35 minutes. Cool in pans 10 minutes; remove to wire racks to cool completely.

4. For frosting, in a metal bowl over simmering water, melt butter and chocolates; stir until smooth. Cool slightly.

5. In a large bowl, combine confectioners' sugar, sour cream and vanilla. Add chocolate mixture; beat until smooth. Spread frosting between the layers and over top and sides of cake. Refrigerate leftovers.

1 PIECE: 685 cal., 29g fat (18g sat. fat), 115mg chol., 505mg sod., 102g carb. (81g sugars, 3g fiber), 7g pro.

HOMEMADE RHUBARB UPSIDE-DOWN CAKE

This light and airy yellow cake is moist but not too sweet, and the caramelized rhubarb topping adds tangy flavor and visual appeal. We like it served with strawberry ice cream.

—Joyce Rowe, Stratham, NH

PREP: 30 MIN. • **BAKE:** 40 MIN. + COOLING • **MAKES:** 12 SERVINGS

⅔ cup packed brown sugar
3 Tbsp. butter, melted
2¼ cups diced fresh or frozen rhubarb
4½ tsp. sugar

BATTER

6 Tbsp. butter, softened
¾ cup sugar
2 large eggs, separated, room temperature
1 tsp. vanilla extract
1 cup plus 2 Tbsp. all-purpose flour
1½ tsp. baking powder
½ tsp. salt
¼ cup 2% milk
¼ tsp. cream of tartar
Whipped cream or vanilla ice cream, optional

1. Preheat oven to 325°. In a small bowl, combine brown sugar and butter. Spread into a greased 10-in. cast-iron or other ovenproof skillet. Layer with rhubarb; sprinkle with sugar. Set aside.

2. In a large bowl, cream butter and sugar until light and fluffy, 5-7 minutes. Beat in egg yolks and vanilla. Combine the flour, baking powder and salt; add to creamed mixture alternately with milk, beating well after each addition.

3. In a small bowl, beat egg whites and cream of tartar on medium speed until stiff peaks form. Gradually fold into the creamed mixture, about ½ cup at a time. Gently spoon over rhubarb.

4. Bake until the cake springs back when lightly touched, 40-50 minutes. Cool for 10 minutes before inverting onto a serving plate. Serve warm, with whipped cream or ice cream if desired.

1 PIECE: 240 cal., 10g fat (6g sat. fat), 59mg chol., 254mg sod., 36g carb. (27g sugars, 1g fiber), 3g pro.

LEMON-LIME BARS

I baked these bars for a luncheon, and a gentleman made his way to the kitchen to compliment the cook who made them.

—Holly Wilkins, Lake Elmore, VT

PREP: 20 MIN. • **BAKE:** 20 MIN. + COOLING • **MAKES:** 4 DOZEN

- **1 cup butter, softened**
- **½ cup confectioners' sugar**
- **2 tsp. grated lime zest**
- **1¾ cups all-purpose flour**
- **¼ tsp. salt**

FILLING

- **4 large eggs**
- **1½ cups sugar**
- **¼ cup all-purpose flour**
- **½ tsp. baking powder**
- **⅓ cup lemon juice**
- **2 tsp. grated lemon zest**
- **Confectioners' sugar**

1. Preheat oven to 350°. In a large bowl, cream butter and confectioners' sugar until light and fluffy, 5-7 minutes. Beat in lime zest. Combine flour and salt; gradually add to creamed mixture and mix well.

2. Press into a greased 13x9-in. baking dish. Bake just until edges are lightly browned, 13-15 minutes.

3. Meanwhile, in another large bowl, beat eggs and sugar. Combine flour and baking powder. Gradually add to egg mixture. Stir in lemon juice and zest; beat until frothy. Pour over hot crust.

4. Bake until light golden brown, 20-25 minutes. Cool on a wire rack. Dust with confectioners' sugar. Cut into squares. Store in the refrigerator.

1 BAR: 88 cal., 4g fat (2g sat. fat), 28mg chol., 60mg sod., 12g carb. (7g sugars, 0 fiber), 1g pro.

KITCHEN TIP: When zesting limes or lemons, remember that the outermost part of a citrus fruit has the most desirable flavor. Be careful not to grate too far down into the peel. The lighter-colored inner part of the peel, the pith, tastes bitter.

STRAWBERRY MASCARPONE CAKE

This cake bakes up high and fluffy, and the berries add a fresh fruity flavor.

—Carol Wit, Tinley Park, IL

PREP: 1 HOUR + CHILLING • BAKE: 30 MIN. + COOLING • MAKES: 12 SERVINGS

- **6 cups fresh strawberries, halved (2 lbs.)**
- **2 Tbsp. sugar**
- **1 tsp. grated orange zest**
- **1 Tbsp. orange juice**
- **½ tsp. almond extract**

CAKE
- **6 large eggs, separated, room temperature**
- **2 cups cake flour**
- **2 tsp. baking powder**
- **¼ tsp. salt**
- **1½ cups sugar, divided**
- **½ cup canola oil**
- **¼ cup water**
- **1 Tbsp. grated orange zest**
- **½ tsp. almond extract**

WHIPPED CREAM
- **2 cups heavy whipping cream**
- **⅓ cup confectioners' sugar**
- **2 tsp. vanilla extract**

FILLING
- **1 cup mascarpone cheese**
- **½ cup heavy whipping cream**

1. In a large bowl, combine the first 5 ingredients. Refrigerate, covered, at least 30 minutes. Meanwhile, place egg whites in a large bowl; let stand at room temperature 30 minutes. Preheat oven to 350°. Grease bottoms of two 8-in. round baking pans; line with parchment. Sift flour, baking powder and salt together twice; place in another large bowl.

2. In a small bowl, whisk egg yolks, 1¼ cups sugar, oil, water, orange zest and almond extract until blended. Add to flour mixture; beat until well blended.

3. With clean beaters, beat egg whites on medium until soft peaks form. Gradually add remaining sugar, 1 Tbsp. at a time, beating on high after each addition until sugar is dissolved. Continue beating until soft glossy peaks form. Fold a fourth of the egg whites into batter, then fold in remaining whites.

4. Gently transfer to prepared pans. Bake on lowest oven rack until top springs back, 30-35 minutes. Cool in pans 10 minutes before removing to wire racks; remove paper. Cool completely.

5. Meanwhile, for whipped cream, in a large bowl, beat cream until it begins to thicken. Add confectioners' sugar and vanilla; beat until soft peaks form. Refrigerate, covered, at least 1 hour. For filling, in a small bowl, beat mascarpone cheese and cream until stiff peaks form. Refrigerate until assembling.

6. Drain strawberries, reserving juice mixture. Using a serrated knife, trim tops of cakes if domed. Place 1 cake layer on a serving plate. Brush with half of reserved juice mixture; spread with ¾ cup filling. Arrange half the strawberries over top, creating an even layer; spread with remaining filling. Brush remaining cake layer with remaining juice mixture; place layer over filling, brushed side down.

7. Gently stir whipped cream; spread over top and sides of cake. Just before serving, arrange remaining strawberries over cake.

1 PIECE: 677 cal., 48g fat (22g sat. fat), 196mg chol., 200mg sod., 56g carb. (36g sugars, 2g fiber), 10g pro.

BUTTERMILK CAKE WITH CARAMEL ICING

So moist and tender, this cake melts in your mouth! It's been a favorite cake recipe of my family since the 1970s and goes over really well at church potluck meals and bake sales.

—Anna Jean Allen, West Liberty, KY

PREP: 35 MIN. • **BAKE:** 45 MIN. + COOLING • **MAKES:** 16 SERVINGS

1 cup butter, softened
2⅓ cups sugar
1½ tsp. vanilla extract
3 large eggs, room temperature
3 cups all-purpose flour
1 tsp. baking powder
½ tsp. baking soda
1 cup buttermilk

ICING

¼ cup butter, cubed
½ cup packed brown sugar
⅓ cup heavy whipping cream
1 cup confectioners' sugar

1. Preheat oven to 350°. Grease and flour a 10-in. fluted tube pan.

2. Cream butter and sugar until light and fluffy, 5-7 minutes. Beat in vanilla; add eggs, 1 at a time, beating well after each addition. In another bowl, whisk together flour, baking powder and baking soda; add to creamed mixture alternately with buttermilk (batter will be thick). Transfer to prepared pan.

3. Bake until a toothpick inserted in center comes out clean, 45-50 minutes. Cool in pan 10 minutes before removing to a wire rack to cool completely.

4. For icing, in a small saucepan, combine butter, brown sugar and cream; bring to a boil over medium heat, stirring constantly. Remove from heat; cool 5-10 minutes. Gradually beat in the confectioners' sugar; spoon over cake.

1 PIECE: 419 cal., 17g fat (11g sat. fat), 79mg chol., 230mg sod., 63g carb. (44g sugars, 1g fiber), 4g pro.

KITCHEN TIP: To remove cakes easily, use solid shortening to grease plain and fluted tube pans.

LODGE

BLUEBERRY DREAM PIE

This showstopping pie can be decorated to fit any season. I like to make stars for Independence Day.

—Kerry Nakayama, New York, NY

PREP: 40 MIN. • BAKE: 35 MIN. + COOLING • MAKES: 8 SERVINGS

Dough for double-crust pie

CHEESE FILLING

- **4 oz. reduced-fat cream cheese**
- **½ cup confectioners' sugar**
- **1 Tbsp. lemon juice**
- **1 large egg yolk, room temperature**

BLUEBERRY FILLING

- **½ cup plus 1 Tbsp. sugar, divided**
- **2 Tbsp. all-purpose flour**
- **1 Tbsp. cornstarch**
- **¼ cup cold water**
- **6 cups fresh or frozen blueberries, divided**
- **2 Tbsp. lemon juice**
- **1 Tbsp. minced fresh mint or 1 tsp. dried mint**
- **1 large egg white, beaten**

1. On a floured surface, roll each dough disk to fit a 9-in. cast-iron skillet or deep-dish pie plate. Line with bottom crust. Trim crust to ½ in. beyond edge of skillet; flute edges. Line unpricked crust with a double thickness of heavy-duty foil. Bake at 450° for 8 minutes. Remove the foil; bake 5 minutes longer. Cool on a wire rack. Reduce heat to 375°.

2. In a small bowl, beat the cream cheese, confectioners' sugar and lemon juice until light and fluffy. Beat in egg yolk until blended. Spread into crust.

3. In a large saucepan, combine ½ cup sugar, flour and cornstarch; stir in water until smooth. Stir in 2 cups berries. Bring to a boil; cook and stir until thickened, 1-2 minutes. Cool slightly. Gently stir in the lemon juice, mint and remaining berries. Pour over cheese filling.

4. Cut decorative cutouts from remaining crust; arrange over filling, leaving center uncovered. Brush crust with egg white; sprinkle with remaining sugar.

5. Bake at 375° until crust is golden brown and filling is bubbly, 35-40 minutes. If necessary, cover edges with foil during the last 15 minutes to prevent overbrowning. Cool on a wire rack. Refrigerate leftovers.

1 PIECE: 442 cal., 18g fat (8g sat. fat), 46mg chol., 269mg sod., 67g carb. (35g sugars, 3g fiber), 5g pro.

DOUGH FOR DOUBLE-CRUST PIE: Combine 2½ cups all-purpose flour and ½ tsp. salt; cut in 1 cup cold butter until crumbly. Gradually add ⅓-⅔ cup ice water, tossing with a fork until the dough holds together when pressed. Divide dough in half. Shape each into a disk; wrap and refrigerate 1 hour.

CARAMEL FLUFF & TOFFEE TRIFLE

The best part of this stunning dessert is you need just five ingredients to put it together.

—Daniel Anderson, Kenosha, WI

PREP: 15 MIN. + CHILLING • **MAKES:** 12 SERVINGS

- **2 cups heavy whipping cream**
- **¾ cup packed brown sugar**
- **1 tsp. vanilla extract**
- **1 prepared angel food cake (8 to 10 oz.), cut into 1-in. cubes**
- **1 cup milk chocolate English toffee bits**

SERVE WITH:
Chicken Marsala Lasagna, Page 127

1. In a large bowl, beat the cream, brown sugar and vanilla just until blended. Refrigerate, covered, 20 minutes. Beat until stiff peaks form.

2. In a 4-qt. glass bowl, layer one-third of each of the following: cake cubes, whipped cream and toffee bits. Repeat layers twice. Refrigerate until serving.

1 SERVING: 347 cal., 22g fat (13g sat. fat), 61mg chol., 227mg sod., 38g carb. (27g sugars, 0 fiber), 2g pro.

BERRY-PATCH BROWNIE PIZZA

I just love the combination of fruit, almonds and chocolate that makes this brownie so unique. The fruit lightens the chocolate a bit and makes it feel as though you are eating something sinfully healthy.

—Sue Kauffman, Columbia City, IN

PREP: 20 MIN. + CHILLING • **BAKE:** 15 MIN. + COOLING • **MAKES:** 12 SERVINGS

- **1 pkg. fudge brownie mix (13x9-in. pan size)**
- **⅓ cup chopped unblanched almonds**
- **1 tsp. almond extract**

TOPPING

- **1 pkg. (8 oz.) cream cheese, softened**
- **1 Tbsp. sugar**
- **1 tsp. vanilla extract**
- **½ tsp. grated lemon zest**
- **2 cups whipped topping**
- **Assorted fresh berries**
- **Optional: Fresh mint leaves and coarse sugar**

1. Preheat oven to 375°. Prepare brownie batter according to package directions for fudgelike brownies, adding almonds and almond extract. Spread into a greased 14-in. pizza pan.

2. Bake until a toothpick inserted in center comes out clean, 15-18 minutes. Cool completely on a wire rack.

3. Beat first 4 topping ingredients until smooth; fold in whipped topping. Spread over crust to within ½ in. of edges; refrigerate, loosely covered, 2 hours.

4. To serve, cut into 12 slices; top with berries of choice. If desired, top with mint and sprinkle with coarse sugar.

1 PIECE: 404 cal., 26g fat (8g sat. fat), 51mg chol., 240mg sod., 39g carb. (26g sugars, 2g fiber), 5g pro.

APPLE BUTTER CAKE ROLL

This spicy gingerbread cake is a new take on a classic pumpkin roll. It might make you think back fondly to your grandma's kitchen.

—Debbie White, Williamson, WV

PREP: 35 MIN. • **BAKE:** 15 MIN. + CHILLING • **MAKES:** 15 SERVINGS

- **3 large eggs, separated**
- **1 cup all-purpose flour, divided**
- **2 Tbsp. plus ½ cup sugar, divided**
- **2 tsp. ground cinnamon**
- **1 tsp. baking powder**
- **1 tsp. ground ginger**
- **1 tsp. ground cloves**
- **¼ tsp. baking soda**
- **¼ cup butter, melted**
- **¼ cup molasses**
- **2 Tbsp. water**
- **1 Tbsp. confectioners' sugar**
- **2 cups apple butter**

1. Preheat oven to 375°. Place egg whites in a small bowl; let stand at room temperature for 30 minutes. Line a greased 15x10x1-in. baking pan with waxed paper and grease the paper. Sprinkle with 1 Tbsp. flour and 2 Tbsp. sugar; set aside.

2. In a large bowl, combine remaining flour and sugar; add the cinnamon, baking powder, ginger, cloves and baking soda. In another bowl, whisk the egg yolks, butter, molasses and water. Add to dry ingredients and beat until blended. Beat egg whites on medium speed until soft peaks form; fold into batter. Pour into prepared pan.

3. Bake for 12-14 minutes or until cake springs back when lightly touched. Cool for 5 minutes. Turn cake onto a kitchen towel dusted with confectioners' sugar. Gently peel off waxed paper. Roll up cake in the towel jelly-roll style, starting with a short side. Cool completely on a wire rack.

4. Unroll the cake; spread the apple butter to within ½ in. of edges. Roll up again. Cover and chill for 1 hour before serving. Refrigerate leftovers.

1 PIECE: 186 cal., 4g fat (2g sat. fat), 45mg chol., 100mg sod., 35g carb. (26g sugars, 1g fiber), 2g pro.

DIABETIC EXCHANGES: 2 starch, 1 fat.

A TASTE TO REMEMBER

BY KAREN GIEBEL, REPUBLIC, WASHINGTON

Have you ever seen something out of the blue that brings back a quick flood of memories? It happened to me when I was living in Germany a few years ago, and I thought back to my childhood in New York State, my dad, and the black raspberries he grew.

On my morning walk I spotted some berries growing alongside a fence. Upon closer inspection I saw that they were plump blackberries—not the same as the black raspberries of my youth, but similar—and so I hurried home across the pasture to get a bowl and start picking before yellow jackets discovered them.

As I picked berries that morning, I could almost hear my dad saying to my mom, "Clare, it's 8 o'clock. Aren't those kids up yet? We have to get the raspberries picked."

In New York, black raspberries ripen in July; since it was during summer vacation, I wanted to sleep in. But as any farmer will tell you, berries need to be picked before the sun dries the dew and they start to shrivel up.

That meant I was hustled out of my bed, given a stack of quart-size baskets and sent out to the rows. To my young eyes the rows looked endless, but it was an easy job a 10-year-old could handle. And, being a short little kid, I did not have to bend over to look for the biggest and best-hidden fruit!

One berry in the basket and one in my mouth, one in the basket and one in my mouth—I just loved popping the seeds with my teeth and then tasting the juicy sweetness of the shiny black gems.

I knew my mom would be inside making black raspberry jam, which to this day is my favorite. She froze the raspberries in quart containers, just the right size for pie-making later. And every summer she made at least one black raspberry pie and a black raspberry cobbler, too.

Eventually friends would wander over and then the berry wars would begin, all of us throwing the berries across the tops of the bushes, aiming to turn each other purple with berry juice. I'm sorry to think about all of the fruit we wasted! Black raspberries today, if you can find them, cost their weight in gold. Back then, Dad put them out on a table at the roadside where they sold for 45 cents a quart.

As I reminisced while picking from this lovely wild berry patch, I found myself wishing with all my heart that my dad, Bill Castleberry, was standing there again right outside my bedroom window saying to Mom, "Clare, it's 8 o'clock. Aren't those kids up yet?"

Craving some berries right about now? Try Berry Bliss Cobbler (at left). The recipe is on page 314.

BERRY BLISS COBBLER

A little bit sweet, a little bit tart and topped off with golden sugar-kissed biscuits, this cobbler is summer perfection.

—Taste of Home *Test Kitchen*

PREP: 10 MIN. + STANDING • **BAKE:** 20 MIN. • **MAKES:** 6 SERVINGS

- **3 cups fresh strawberries, halved**
- **1½ cups fresh raspberries**
- **1½ cups fresh blueberries**
- **⅔ cup plus 1 Tbsp. sugar, divided**
- **3 Tbsp. quick-cooking tapioca**
- **1 cup all-purpose flour**
- **1 Tbsp. sugar**
- **2 tsp. baking powder**
- **¼ tsp. salt**
- **¼ cup cold butter, cubed**
- **1 large egg, room temperature**
- **¼ cup plus 2 Tbsp. 2% milk**
- **Coarse sugar**

1. Preheat oven to 400°. Toss strawberries, raspberries and blueberries with ⅔ cup sugar and tapioca. Transfer to a greased 10-in. cast-iron or other ovenproof skillet; let stand 20 minutes.

2. Meanwhile, whisk flour, 1 Tbsp. sugar, baking powder and salt. Cut in butter until mixture resembles coarse crumbs. In another bowl, whisk together egg and milk; stir into crumb mixture just until moistened. Drop by tablespoonfuls onto fruit. Sprinkle with coarse sugar.

3. Bake, uncovered, until filling is bubbly and topping is golden brown, 20-25 minutes. Serve warm.

1 SERVING: 335 cal., 9g fat (5g sat. fat), 52mg chol., 298mg sod., 60g carb. (34g sugars, 5g fiber), 5g pro.

CAST-IRON PEACH CROSTATA

While the crostata, an open-faced fruit tart, is actually Italian, my version's peach filling is American all the way.

—Lauren McAnelly, Des Moines, IA

PREP: 45 MIN. + CHILLING • **BAKE:** 45 MIN. • **MAKES:** 10 SERVINGS

- **1½ cups all-purpose flour**
- **2 Tbsp. plus ¾ cup packed brown sugar, divided**
- **1¼ tsp. salt, divided**
- **½ cup cold unsalted butter, cubed**
- **2 Tbsp. shortening**
- **3 to 5 Tbsp. ice water**
- **8 cups sliced peaches (about 7-8 medium)**
- **1 Tbsp. lemon juice**
- **3 Tbsp. cornstarch**
- **½ tsp. ground cinnamon**
- **¼ tsp. ground nutmeg**
- **1 large egg, beaten**
- **2 Tbsp. sliced almonds**
- **1 Tbsp. coarse sugar**
- **⅓ cup water**
- **1 cup fresh raspberries, optional**

1. Mix flour, 2 Tbsp. brown sugar and 1 tsp. salt; cut in butter and shortening until crumbly. Gradually add ice water, tossing with a fork until dough holds together when pressed. Shape into a disk. Cover and refrigerate 1 hour or overnight.

2. Combine peaches and lemon juice. Add remaining brown sugar, cornstarch, spices and remaining salt; toss gently. Let stand 30 minutes.

3. Preheat oven to 400°. On a lightly floured surface, roll dough into a 13-in. circle; transfer to a 10-in. cast-iron skillet, letting excess hang over edge. Using a slotted spoon, transfer peaches into crust, reserving liquid. Fold crust edge over filling, pleating as you go, leaving center uncovered. Brush folded crust with beaten egg; sprinkle with almonds and coarse sugar. Bake until crust is dark golden and filling is bubbly, 45-55 minutes.

4. In a small saucepan, combine reserved liquid and water; bring to a boil. Simmer until thickened, 1-2 minutes; serve warm with pie. If desired, top with fresh raspberries.

1 PIECE: 322 cal., 13g fat (7g sat. fat), 43mg chol., 381mg sod., 49g carb. (30g sugars, 3g fiber), 4g pro.

BANANA PUDDING

I didn't see my son for more than two years after he enlisted in the Marines after high school. And when I saw him arrive at the airport, I just grabbed hold of him and burst out crying. When we got home, the first thing he ate was two bowls of my easy banana pudding. He's a true southern boy! It's a dessert, but you can have it for breakfast, lunch or dinner.

—Stephanie Harris, Montpelier, VA

PREP: 35 MIN. + CHILLING • **MAKES:** 9 SERVINGS

- **¾ cup sugar**
- **¼ cup all-purpose flour**
- **¼ tsp. salt**
- **3 cups 2% milk**
- **3 large eggs**
- **1½ tsp. vanilla extract**
- **8 oz. vanilla wafers (about 60 cookies), divided**
- **4 large ripe bananas, cut into ¼-in. slices**

1. In a large saucepan, mix sugar, flour and salt. Whisk in milk. Cook and stir over medium heat until thickened and bubbly. Reduce heat to low; cook and stir 2 minutes longer. Remove from heat.

2. In a small bowl, whisk eggs. Whisk a small amount of hot mixture into eggs; return all to pan, whisking constantly. Bring to a gentle boil; cook and stir 2 minutes. Remove from heat. Stir in vanilla. Cool 15 minutes, stirring occasionally.

3. In an ungreased 8-in. square baking dish, layer 25 vanilla wafers, half of the banana slices and half of the pudding. Repeat the layers.

4. Press plastic wrap onto surface of pudding. Refrigerate 4 hours or overnight. Just before serving, remove wrap; crush remaining wafers and sprinkle over top.

1 SERVING: 302 cal., 7g fat (2g sat. fat), 80mg chol., 206mg sod., 55g carb. (37g sugars, 2g fiber), 7g pro.

KITCHEN TIP: A peanut butter drizzle and chopped salted peanuts take this old-time country dessert to a new level.

LODGE

CHOCOLATE PECAN SKILLET COOKIE

Bake up the ultimate shareable cookie. For variety, swap out the chocolate chips for an equal quantity of M&M's or chocolate chunks. Or go super fancy by mixing the chocolate chips and pecans into the dough, then gently folding in 1½ cups fresh raspberries.

—James Schend, Pleasant Prairie, WI

PREP: 15 MIN. • **BAKE:** 35 MIN. • **MAKES:** 12 SERVINGS

- **1 cup butter**
- **1 cup sugar**
- **1 cup packed brown sugar**
- **2 large eggs, room temperature**
- **2 tsp. vanilla extract**
- **3 cups all-purpose flour**
- **1½ tsp. baking soda**
- **½ tsp. kosher salt**
- **1 cup 60% cacao bittersweet chocolate baking chips**
- **1 cup chopped pecans, toasted**
- **Vanilla ice cream, optional**

1. Preheat oven to 350°. In a 12-in. cast-iron skillet, heat butter in oven as it preheats. Meanwhile, in a large bowl, stir together sugar and brown sugar. When butter is almost melted, remove skillet from oven and swirl butter until completely melted. Stir butter into sugar mixture; set skillet aside.

2. Beat eggs and vanilla into sugar mixture. In another bowl, whisk together flour, baking soda and salt; gradually beat into sugar mixture. Stir in chocolate chips and nuts. Spread mixture into buttered skillet.

3. Bake until toothpick inserted in center comes out with moist crumbs and top is golden brown, 35-40 minutes. Serve warm, with vanilla ice cream if desired.

1 SERVING: 528 cal., 27g fat (13g sat. fat), 72mg chol., 378mg sod., 69g carb. (43g sugars, 3g fiber), 6g pro.

KITCHEN TIP: This cookie may be prepared in four 6-in. cast-iron skillets. Just brush skillets with melted butter before adding dough. Bake 25-30 minutes.

MAPLE WALNUT CAKE

This cake reminds me of my beloved grandpa, who made delicious maple syrup when I was a child. This cake honors his memory, and has proven to be a favorite with family and friends.

—Lori Fee, Middlesex, NY

PREP: 45 MIN. • **BAKE:** 15 MIN. + COOLING • **MAKES:** 16 SERVINGS

- **½ cup unsalted butter, softened**
- **1½ cups packed light brown sugar**
- **3 large eggs, room temperature**
- **1 tsp. maple flavoring or maple syrup**
- **2 cups all-purpose flour**
- **1 tsp. baking powder**
- **1 tsp. baking soda**
- **¼ tsp. salt**
- **1 cup buttermilk**

CANDIED WALNUTS

- **1 Tbsp. unsalted butter**
- **1½ cups coarsely chopped walnuts**
- **1 Tbsp. maple syrup**
- **¼ tsp. salt**

FROSTING

- **2 cups unsalted butter, softened**
- **1 tsp. maple flavoring or maple syrup**
- **¼ tsp. salt**
- **5 cups confectioners' sugar**
- **¼ to ½ cup half-and-half cream**
- **3 Tbsp. maple syrup, divided**

1. Preheat oven to 350°. Line bottoms of 3 greased 9-in. round baking pans with parchment; grease parchment.

2. Cream the butter and brown sugar until light and fluffy, 5-7 minutes. Add eggs, 1 at a time, beating well after each addition. Beat in the maple flavoring. In another bowl, whisk together flour, baking powder, baking soda and salt; add to creamed mixture alternately with buttermilk, beating after each addition.

3. Transfer to prepared pans. Bake until a toothpick inserted in center comes out clean, 11-13 minutes. Cool in pans 10 minutes before removing to wire racks; remove paper. Cool completely.

4. For candied walnuts, in a large skillet, melt the butter over medium heat; saute walnuts until toasted, about 5 minutes. Stir in maple syrup and salt; cook and stir 1 minute. Spread onto foil; cool completely.

5. For frosting, beat butter until creamy. Beat in maple flavoring and salt. Gradually beat in confectioners' sugar and enough cream to reach desired consistency.

6. Place 1 cake layer on a serving plate; spread with 1 cup frosting. Sprinkle with ½ cup candied walnuts and drizzle with 1 Tbsp. maple syrup. Repeat layers.

7. Top with remaining layer. Frost top and sides of cake. Top with remaining walnuts and syrup.

1 PIECE: 653 cal., 38g fat (20g sat. fat), 116mg chol., 275mg sod., 75g carb. (61g sugars, 1g fiber), 5g pro.

CITRUS MERINGUE PIE

Thanks to orange and lemon, this lovely pie packs a bold sweet-tart flavor.

—Barbara Carlucci, Orange Park, FL

PREP: 30 MIN. • **BAKE:** 15 MIN. + CHILLING • **MAKES:** 8 SERVINGS

Dough for single-crust pie (9 in.)
- **1 cup sugar**
- **5 Tbsp. cornstarch**
- **½ tsp. salt**
- **1 cup water**
- **1 cup orange juice**
- **4 large egg yolks**
- **½ cup lemon juice**
- **2 Tbsp. butter**
- **1 tsp. grated lemon zest**
- **1 tsp. grated orange zest**

MERINGUE
- **4 large egg whites**
- **1 tsp. vanilla extract**
- **¼ tsp. cream of tartar**
- **½ cup sugar**

1. Preheat oven to 450°. On a lightly floured surface, roll dough to a ⅛-in.-thick circle; transfer to a 9-in. pie plate. Trim crust to ½ in. beyond rim of plate; flute edge. Line unpricked crust with a double thickness of foil. Fill with pie weights or dried beans.

2. Bake until bottom is lightly browned, 8-10 minutes. Remove foil and weights; bake until golden brown, 5-8 minutes longer. Cool on a wire rack. Reduce oven temperature to 350°.

3. In a large saucepan, mix sugar, cornstarch and salt. Whisk in water and orange juice. Cook and stir over medium-high heat until thickened and bubbly. Reduce heat to low; cook and stir 2 minutes longer (mixture will be thick). Remove from heat.

4. In a small bowl, whisk a small amount of hot mixture into egg yolks; return all to pan, whisking constantly. Bring to a gentle boil; cook and stir 2 minutes. Remove from heat. Gently stir in lemon juice, butter, and lemon and orange zests.

5. For meringue, in a large bowl, beat egg whites with vanilla and cream of tartar on medium speed until foamy. Add sugar, 1 Tbsp. at a time, beating on high after each addition until sugar is dissolved. Continue beating until soft glossy peaks form.

6. Transfer hot filling to crust. Spread meringue over filling, sealing to edge of crust; swirl top with the back of a spoon.

7. Bake until meringue is golden brown, 13-16 minutes. Cool on a wire rack for 1 hour. Chill pie 3 hours before serving. Refrigerate leftovers.

1 PIECE: 415 cal., 17g fat (10g sat. fat), 140mg chol., 318mg sod., 62g carb. (41g sugars, 1g fiber), 6g pro.

DOUGH FOR A SINGLE-CRUST PIE: Combine 1¼ cups of all-purpose flour and ¼ tsp. salt; cut in ½ cup cold butter until crumbly. Gradually add 3-5 Tbsp. ice water, tossing with a fork until dough holds together when pressed. Cover and refrigerate 1 hour.

STRAWBERRY-CHOCOLATE MERINGUE TORTE

I make this rich and delicious torte whenever I'm asked to bring dessert to any occasion. Use reduced-calorie whipped topping to create a lighter version.

—Christine McCullough, Auburn, MA

PREP: 45 MIN. • **BAKE:** 70 MIN. + COOLING • **MAKES:** 6 SERVINGS

- **4 large egg whites**
- **3 cups sliced fresh strawberries**
- **1 tsp. plus 1 cup sugar, divided**
- **1½ cups heavy whipping cream**
- **⅓ cup confectioners' sugar**
- **¾ tsp. vanilla extract**
- **¼ tsp. cream of tartar**
- **¼ tsp. salt**
- **½ cup semisweet chocolate chips**

1. Place the egg whites in a large bowl; let stand at room temperature 30 minutes. Meanwhile, in a small bowl, combine strawberries and 1 tsp. sugar. In another bowl, beat cream until it begins to thicken. Add confectioners' sugar and vanilla; beat until soft peaks form. Refrigerate strawberries and whipped cream, covered, until assembly.

2. Preheat oven to 250°. Line a baking sheet with parchment. Trace two 8-in. circles 1 in. apart on paper; set aside. Add cream of tartar and salt to egg whites; beat on medium speed until foamy. Gradually add remaining sugar, 1 Tbsp. at a time, beating on high after each addition until sugar is dissolved. Continue beating until stiff glossy peaks form. Spread evenly over circles.

3. Bake until set and dry, 70-80 minutes. Turn off oven (do not open oven door); leave meringues in oven 1½ hours. Remove from oven; cool completely.

4. In a microwave, melt chocolate chips; stir until smooth. Spread evenly over tops of meringues. Carefully remove one meringue to a serving plate. Remove whipped cream from refrigerator; beat until stiff peaks form. Spread half of the whipped cream over the meringue; top with half of the strawberries. Repeat layers. Serve immediately.

1 PIECE: 470 cal., 26g fat (16g sat. fat), 68mg chol., 154mg sod., 58g carb. (54g sugars, 2g fiber), 5g pro.

MIXED FRUIT SHORTCAKES

This delightful downsized recipe makes just two biscuitlike shortcakes. Fill them with fresh fruit of your choice and top with whipped cream for an impressive dinner finale. Need more servings? The recipe is easy to double or triple for larger dinners.

—Sue Ross, Casa Grande, AZ

TAKES: 30 MIN. • **MAKES:** 2 SERVINGS

1 cup mixed fresh berries
½ cup sliced fresh peaches or nectarines
4 tsp. sugar, divided
½ cup all-purpose flour
¾ tsp. baking powder
⅛ tsp. salt
2 Tbsp. shortening
3 Tbsp. 2% milk
Whipped cream

1. In a small bowl, combine the berries, peaches and 2 tsp. sugar; set aside. In another bowl, combine the flour, baking powder and salt; cut in shortening until mixture is crumbly. Stir in milk just until moistened. Drop by lightly packed ⅓ cupfuls 2 in. apart onto an ungreased baking sheet. Gently flatten into 2½-in. circles. Sprinkle with remaining sugar.

2. Bake at 425° for 10-12 minutes or until golden brown. Remove to a wire rack to cool. Split the shortcakes in half horizontally. Spoon fruit onto bottoms; spread whipped cream over fruit or on the shortcake tops.

1 SERVING: 329 cal., 13g fat (3g sat. fat), 2mg chol., 311mg sod., 48g carb. (20g sugars, 5g fiber), 5g pro.

EASY NUTELLA CHEESECAKE

Creamy chocolate-hazelnut spread tops a crust made of crushed Oreo cookies to make this irresistible baked cheesecake.

—Nick Iverson, Denver, CO

PREP: 35 MIN. • **BAKE:** 1¼ HOURS + CHILLING • **MAKES:** 16 SERVINGS

- **2½ cups lightly crushed Oreo cookies (about 24 cookies)**
- **¼ cup sugar**
- **¼ cup butter, melted**

FILLING

- **4 pkg. (8 oz. each) cream cheese, softened**
- **½ cup sugar**
- **2 jars (26½ oz. each) Nutella**
- **1 cup heavy whipping cream**
- **1 tsp. salt**
- **4 large eggs, room temperature, lightly beaten**
- **½ cup chopped hazelnuts, toasted**

1. Preheat oven to 325°. Pulse cookies and sugar in a food processor until fine crumbs form. Continue processing while gradually adding butter in a steady stream. Press mixture onto bottom of a greased 10x3-in. springform pan. Securely wrap the bottom and sides of springform in a double thickness of heavy-duty foil (about 18 in. square).

2. For filling, beat cream cheese and sugar until smooth. Beat in Nutella, cream and salt. Add eggs; beat on low speed just until blended. Pour over crust.

3. Bake until a thermometer inserted in center reads 160°, about 1¼ hours. Cool 1¼ hours on a wire rack. Refrigerate overnight, covering when completely cooled.

4. Gently loosen sides from pan with a knife; remove rim. Top cheesecake with chopped hazelnuts.

1 PIECE: 900 cal., 62g fat (22g sat. fat), 129mg chol., 478mg sod., 84g carb. (71g sugars, 4g fiber), 12g pro.

BLACKBERRY CRISP

I adapted this comforting dessert from a recipe my mother-in-law gave to me. Hers fed a family with nine growing kids who were never full, so there was never any left. There aren't any leftovers when I make my downsized version, either!

—Marliss Lee, Independence, MO

PREP: 15 MIN. • **BAKE:** 20 MIN. • **MAKES:** 2 SERVINGS

- **2 cups fresh or frozen blackberries**
- **2 Tbsp. sugar**
- **1 tsp. cornstarch**
- **1½ tsp. water**
- **½ tsp. lemon juice**
- **½ cup quick-cooking oats**
- **¼ cup all-purpose flour**
- **¼ cup packed brown sugar**
- **½ tsp. ground cinnamon**
- **¼ cup cold butter**
- **Vanilla ice cream**

1. Place blackberries in a greased 1-qt. baking dish. In a small bowl, combine the sugar, cornstarch, water and lemon juice until smooth. Pour over berries. Combine the oats, flour, brown sugar and cinnamon; cut in butter until crumbly. Sprinkle over the berries.

2. Bake, uncovered, at 375° until filling is bubbly, 20-25 minutes. Serve warm with ice cream.

1¼ CUPS: 576 cal., 25g fat (14g sat. fat), 61mg chol., 245mg sod., 87g carb. (54g sugars, 6g fiber), 6g pro.

EVEN MORE DOWNHOME FARMHOUSE FAMILY DINNERS

Whether you're hosting a special night or simply craving a home-cooked specialty, turn here for 30 additional menus, each sure to make mealtime memories.

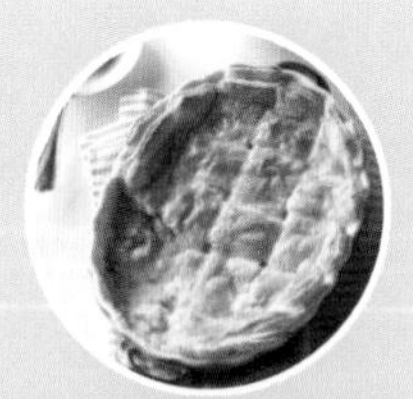

HEARTWARMING POTPIE

- Puff Pastry Chicken Potpie, p. 139
- Easy Batter Rolls, p. 228
- Refreshing Raspberry Iced Tea, p. 15
- Chocolate Pecan Skillet Cookie, p. 319

TRADITIONAL HAM FEAST

- Cider-Glazed Ham, p. 183
- Honey-Lemon Asparagus, p. 64
- Swiss Cheese Bread, p. 111
- Mixed Berry Tiramisu, p. 112

CASUAL & COMFORTING

- Broccoli Beer Cheese Soup, p. 39
- Soft Beer Pretzel Nuggets, p. 287
- Spinach Salad with Poppy Seed Dressing, p. 32
- Easy Nutella Cheesecake, p. 328

MEAT LOVERS MEAL

- Peppery Roast Beef, p. 77
- Herbed Harvest Vegetable Casserole, p. 227
- Overnight Yeast Rolls, p. 14
- Southern Sweet Potato Tart, p. 29

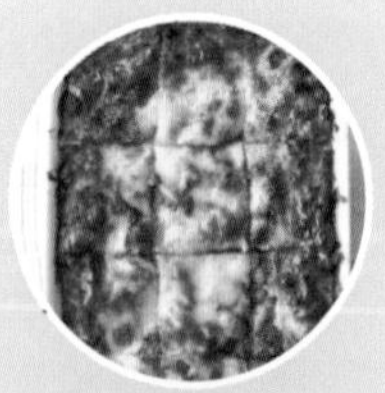

HEARTY LASAGNA DINNER

- Sausage Lasagna, p. 99
- Parmesan Garlic Breadsticks, p. 251
- Red & Green Salad with Toasted Almonds, p. 216
- Caramel Fluff & Toffee Trifle, p. 306

FUN & FESTIVE FISH

- Pretzel-Crusted Catfish, p. 172
- Ribbon Salad with Orange Vinaigrette p. 213
- Smoky Macaroni & Cheese, p. 272
- Citrus Meringue Pie, p. 323

COZY CHICKEN LINEUP

- Apple Barbecue Chicken, p. 180
- Parmesan Baked Potatoes, p. 65
- Fresh Sugar Snap Pea Salad, p. 86
- Apple Butter Cake Roll, p. 310

SIMMERING SUPPER

- Slow-Cooked Beef Brisket, p. 187
- Chive Smashed Potatoes, p. 232
- Oven-Fried Cornbread, p. 48
- Banana Pudding, p. 316

HEARTY PORK ROAST

- Apple Roasted Pork with Cherry Balsamic Glaze, p. 188
- Glazed Baby Carrots, p. 231
- Sweet Potato Crescents, p. 239
- Autumn Apple Torte, p. 44

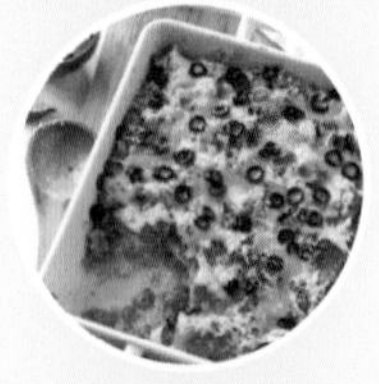

FULL-FLAVORED FAVORITES

- Tamale Pie, p. 147
- Chip-Crusted Grilled Corn, p. 279
- Agua de Jamaica, p. 58
- Homemade Churros, p. 275

EASY SEAFOOD DINNER

- No-Fuss Fish Packets, p. 115
- Italian Pinwheel Rolls, p. 103
- Kale Caesar Salad, p. 20
- Lemon-Lime Bars, p. 298

MEAT & POTATO LOVERS LINEUP

- Grilled Tender Flank Steak, p. 161
- Scalloped Potatoes with Mushrooms, p. 87
- Roasted Red Pepper Green Beans, p. 78
- Homemade Rhubarb Upside-Down Cake, p. 297

IMPRESSIVE TURKEY DINNER

- Juicy Roast Turkey, p. 25
- Almond Broccoli Salad, p. 27
- Mom's Sweet Potato Bake, p. 223
- Maple Walnut Cake, p. 320

HOMEY FRIED CHICKEN

- Best-Ever Fried Chicken, p. 19
- Southern Buttermilk Biscuits, p. 23
- Eddie's Favorite Fiesta Corn, p. 54
- Favorite Chocolate-Bourbon Pecan Tart, p. 50

SUNDAY POT ROAST

- Balsamic Braised Pot Roast, p. 148
- Old-World Rye Bread, p. 95
- Roasted Apple Salad with Spicy Maple-Cider Vinaigrette, p. 40
- Buttermilk Cake with Caramel Icing, p. 302

TEX-MEX CHANGE-UP

- Tex-Mex Meat Loaf, p. 69
- Texas Pecan Rice, p. 243
- Zucchini in Dill Cream Sauce, p. 240
- Lemon Curd-Filled Angel Food Cake, p. 88

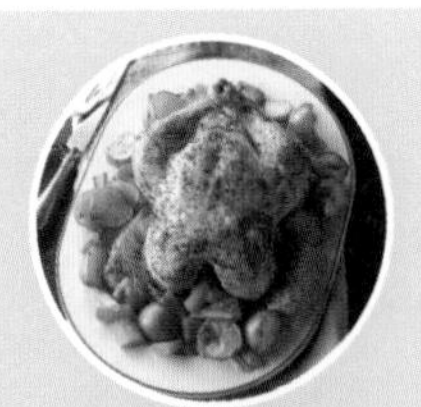

IMPRESSIVE CHICKEN DINNER

- Citrus-Herb Roast Chicken, p. 196
- Whole Wheat French Bread, p. 33
- Garden Salad with Chickpeas, p. 252
- Sandy's Chocolate Cake, p. 294

SUMMERTIME FLAVOR

- Peach-Glazed Ribs, p. 200
- Emily's Honey Lime Coleslaw, p. 235
- Baked Beans Mole, p. 247
- Raspberry Rumble, p. 66

HERB-INFUSED DELIGHTS

- Thyme & Basil Pork Roast, p. 63
- Caraway Cheese Bread, p. 43
- Spinach & Tortellini Soup, p. 236
- Chocolate & Coconut Cream Torte, p. 16

SAVORY SUPPER

- Tilapia with Corn Salsa, p. 143
- Tomato Cheese Bread, p. 283
- Green Salad with Berries, p. 116
- Shortcut Tres Leches Cake, p. 74

CLASSICS MADE EASY

- Glazed Smoked Chops with Pears, p. 132
- Old-World Rye Bread, p. 95
- Creamy Root Veggie Soup, p. 220
- Carrot Blueberry Cupcakes, p. 120

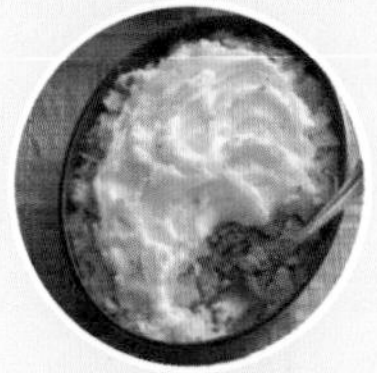

OLD-WORLD CHARM

- Pork Shepherd's Pie, p. 91
- Lemon Artichoke Romaine Salad, p. 108
- Olive & Onion Quick Bread, p. 259
- Old-Fashioned Fruit Compote, p. 271

WEEKNIGHT DELIGHT

- Beef & Bacon Gnocchi Skillet, p. 128
- Cheese & Garlic Biscuits, p. 119
- Sweet Tea Boysenberry Shandy, p. 49
- Lemon Gelato, p. 289

COUNTRY TASTES & TREATS

- Country-Fried Steak, p. 204
- Traditional Mashed Potatoes, p. 20
- Garlic-Herb Pattypan Squash, p. 92
- White Almond No-Bake Cookies, p. 268

PICNIC-PERFECT BUFFET

- Grilled Roast Beef, p. 192
- Red, White & Blue Summer Salad, p. 244
- Simple au Gratin Potatoes, p. 210
- Maple-Glazed Green Beans, p. 256

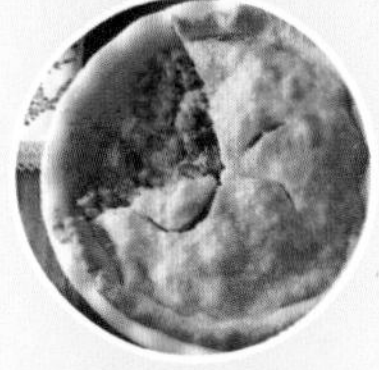

COOL-WEATHER WARMUP

- Spicy Beef & Bean Pie, p. 179
- Ribbon Salad with Orange Vinaigrette, p. 213
- Honey-Lemon Asparagus, p. 64
- Autumn Apple Torte, p. 44

WEEKEND SEAFOOD SUPPER

- Frogmore Stew, p. 47
- Kale Caesar Salad, p. 20
- Dutch-Oven Bread, p. 219
- Creamy Caramel Mocha, p. 276

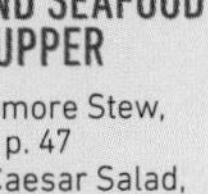

CHANGE-OF-PACE DINNER

- Chicken-Stuffed Cubanelle Peppers, p. 184
- Spicy Pork & Green Chili Verde, p. 57
- Oven-Fried Cornbread, p. 48
- Cinnamon Chip Chai-Spiced Snickerdoodles, p. 280

MUST-TRY WALLEYE

- Crunchy-Coated Walleye, p. 162
- Spinach Salad with Poppy Seed Dressing, p. 32
- Raw Cauliflower Tabbouleh, p. 81
- Mixed Fruit Shortcakes, p. 327

SHEET-PAN SUPPER

- Sliced Ham with Roasted Veggies, p. 124
- Sweet Onion Pimiento Cheese Deviled Eggs, p. 290
- Herbed Feta Dip, p. 262
- Strawberry Chocolate Meringue Torte, p. 324

RECIPE INDEX

A

B

C

D

E